ECCLESIASTES
FROM START2FINISH

MICHAEL WHITWORTH

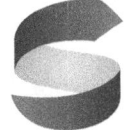

© 2025 by Start2Finish

All rights reserved. No part of this publication may be reproduced, stored in a retrieval system, or transmitted in any form or by any means without the prior written permission of the author. The only exception is brief quotations in printed reviews.

ISBN 978-1-944704-08-7

Published by Start2Finish
Bend, Oregon 97702
start2finish.org

Printed in the United States of America

Unless otherwise noted, all Scripture quotations are from The Holy Bible, English Standard Version®, copyright © 2001 by Crossway Bibles, a publishing ministry of Good News Publishers. Used by permission. All rights reserved.

Cover Design: Evangela Creative

CONTENTS

1.	The Endless Chase	5
2.	When Success Isn't Enough	13
3.	A Season for Everything	21
4.	Better Together (and Sometimes Not)	29
5.	Guard Your Steps	37
6.	The Unfulfilled Life	45
7.	When Good Sense Meets Hard Life	53
8.	When Wicked Men Win	61
9.	Eat, Drink, & Remember	69
10.	Wisdom in the Streets	77
11.	Cast Your Bread	85
12.	Before the Silver Cord Breaks	93

1

THE ENDLESS CHASE

ECCLESIASTES 1

Objective: To understand life's futility under the sun and learn to find joy through humble faith.

INTRODUCTION

A man once spent decades building his dream home—a lakefront masterpiece with hand-carved beams, imported stone, and every comfort money could buy. When the last nail was driven, he stood on the porch and waited for the feeling he'd imagined all those years. It never came. The house was magnificent, but the satisfaction vanished like breath on glass. The next morning he started planning his next project.

That story could have been written by the Teacher of Ecclesiastes. From the opening line, Ecclesiastes confronts our restless hearts with a jarring refrain: "Vanity of vanities! All is vanity." The author is not bitter, only honest. Life under the sun, he says, refuses to yield lasting profit. Work, wisdom, pleasure, legacy—each promise dissolves into mist.

Ecclesiastes is not a book for the cynical but for the sincere—the ones who have tried everything and still feel something missing. Ecclesiastes does not offer cheap comfort; the author dismantles illusions so we can finally receive joy as a gift, not a reward. Before we reach his conclusion—"Fear God and keep his commandments"—we must first walk through his lament. Lesson 1 begins there, in the mirror of our own striving, where we learn that chasing the wind always leaves us empty-handed.

EXAMINATION

Ecclesiastes opens with the voice of Qohelet, a title meaning "Gatherer" or "Assembler." The term may describe one who gathers people to speak wisdom or one who gathers wisdom itself. Though Solomon's name never appears, the superscription evokes his legacy: "a son of David, king in Jerusalem." This kingly voice lends authority but also irony—Solomon, famed for wisdom and wealth, becomes a cautionary example of how little both can guarantee. The supposed master of everything discovers that nothing lasts.

"Vanity of vanities" (1:2)

The theme statement comes first: "Vanity of vanities, says Qohelet, vanity of vanities! All is vanity." The Hebrew word *hebel* means "breath," "vapor," or "mist." It pictures something fleeting, insubstantial, impossible to grasp. Qohelet's verdict is not that life is meaningless, but that it is unmanageable—we can't make it behave. Everything that seems solid slips through our fingers.

This is the lens for the entire book. Life is real but elusive; joy exists but can't be bottled. The word *hebel* captures the frustration of living in a world where the rules don't always work and where certainty evaporates as soon as we think we've caught it.

What profit under the sun? (1:3)

The first question sets the tone for the whole journey: "What advantage does a person have in all his toil under the sun?" The key words here are *yitrôn* ("profit," "gain") and ⬚*āmāl* ("toil," "wearisome labor"). Qohelet's concern is not whether work is good but whether it gives any ultimate surplus. Does it produce anything that endures?

"Under the sun" occurs nearly thirty times and defines the Teacher's field of observation—life from a purely human perspective, within the boundaries of time and mortality. His search will stay within this horizon. He will test whether anything in this world alone, without appeal to eternity, can satisfy the heart.

Routines of creation (1:4–7)

To prove his point, Qohelet turns to creation itself. Generations come and go, but the earth remains. The sun rises and sets, endlessly cycling back to its starting point. The wind turns from north to south and back again, always in motion but never arriving. Rivers rush to the sea, yet the sea is never full.

Nature is tireless but unprogressive. The verbs repeat like gears turning: goes, comes, turns, returns. Creation hums with movement but achieves no surplus. Humanity, too, runs on this treadmill—working, aging, repeating patterns that yield no lasting advantage.

Qohelet's imagery is not cynical but sobering. The beauty of the world hides a relentless sameness. We may enjoy the rhythm, but we cannot change it. The sun will rise tomorrow with or without us.

Words, eyes, and ears (1:8)

"All things are wearisome; no one can speak it." The phrase could also mean "all words are wearying." Either way, Qohelet laments exhaustion. There is no end to what we can say, see, or hear, yet nothing satisfies. Human curiosity and communication mirror nature's cycles—constant, repetitive, hungry.

The more we talk, the less we say; the more we experience, the less we feel fulfilled. Qohelet's world is full of motion but short on meaning. His point is not anti-knowledge but anti-illusion: endless observation and explanation cannot finally capture life's mystery.

Nothing new under the sun (1:9–10)

"What has been will be again... there is nothing new under the sun." Every supposed breakthrough is a remix of something forgotten. Humanity prides itself on progress, but mortality remains unsolved. The wheel turns, technology changes, and yet the same fears, sins, and ambitions persist.

Qohelet's statement challenges both secular optimism and religious formula. Wisdom does not guarantee success; righteousness does not guarantee reward. History, viewed "under the sun," repeats without climax. Only God can make something truly new, but Qohelet will not reach that conclusion until the end.

No remembrance (1:11)

"There is no remembrance of former things, nor will there be remembrance of later ones." Even memory, humanity's claim to permanence, erodes. Time swallows achievements and names alike. The irony is biting: we work for recognition, yet the future won't recognize us.

Qohelet is not promoting despair; he is dismantling false hope. Legacy cannot deliver immortality. Monuments crumble, books gather dust, and descendants forget. This realism clears space for a new kind of wisdom—one that accepts finitude and still chooses joy.

The royal experiment (1:12-13)

Qohelet now speaks in the first person: "I, the Teacher, was king over Israel in Jerusalem. I set my heart to seek and explore by wisdom all that is done under heaven." The royal voice recalls Solomon, the legendary seeker of wisdom, wealth, and pleasure. Yet instead of boasting of success, Qohelet confesses frustration.

The phrase "seek and explore" suggests systematic investigation. He approaches life like a scientist, surveying every human endeavor—work, pleasure, philosophy, politics—to find lasting meaning. But his verdict comes swiftly: "God has given to the sons of man a grievous task to be busy with." Human striving itself becomes part of the burden. We are creatures wired for curiosity and productivity, yet trapped in cycles we cannot control.

The crooked cannot be made straight (1:14-15)

Qohelet summarizes his findings: "I have seen all the works done under the sun; behold, all is vanity and a chasing after wind." The image of chasing the wind captures both effort and futility—energetic pursuit of something ungraspable.

He continues, "What is crooked cannot be made straight; what is lacking cannot be counted." The world is bent, and human effort cannot repair its shape. Wisdom may recognize the distortions, but recognition does not equal remedy. The Teacher voices the ache of Genesis 3—creation's brokenness and humanity's frustration under it. Life's "crookedness" is moral, social, and existential. The harder we try to fix everything, the more we discover our limits.

The burden of wisdom (1:16–17)

"I said in my heart, 'I have acquired great wisdom, surpassing all who were before me in Jerusalem.'" Qohelet is no cynic born of ignorance; his disillusionment arises from deep experience. He has pursued wisdom to the fullest and found it double-edged. "I applied my heart to know wisdom and to know madness and folly."

Wisdom gives clarity but not comfort. The more insight he gains, the more he perceives life's contradictions. Foolishness may provide temporary escape, but it doesn't heal the wound. Wisdom exposes the pain of understanding—a sorrow unavailable to the simple.

The more you know (1:18)

"For in much wisdom is much vexation, and he who increases knowledge increases pain." The Teacher closes the chapter with one of Scripture's starkest paradoxes. Ignorance may not be bliss, but awareness is heavy. The wise see the world as it truly is—bent, unjust, fleeting—and cannot pretend otherwise. Knowledge multiplies grief because it strips away illusion.

This is not an argument for stupidity but for humility. Wisdom's value remains (2:13–14), but it cannot deliver control or permanence. It is a light that reveals vanity, not a ladder that escapes it. The only way forward is to live wisely within the limits, not to abolish them.

Qohelet's opening chapter functions like an x-ray of the human condition. It exposes our restless motion—building, talking, learning, remembering—as wind chasing wind. Creation's cycles, human toil, and even wisdom itself all testify that life "under the sun" cannot be mastered or made to yield permanent gain. Yet this is not hopeless fatalism. By stripping away illusions of control, Qohelet clears a space for gratitude and reverence. If life is vapor, then every breath is gift. The one who fears God will learn to enjoy life, not because it lasts forever under the sun, but because it comes from the One who reigns above it.

APPLICATION

1. Recognize the limits of control

Qohelet's first sermon invites us to release the illusion that we can master life. We plan, build, and save, yet the world keeps spinning as if our effort were a drop in the ocean. The Teacher's honesty doesn't push us toward despair but toward surrender. The wise person accepts limits as part of faith. When we acknowledge that the crooked cannot be straightened by our own power, we stop confusing control with responsibility. Our task is to act faithfully within the boundaries God gives, not to guarantee results. Every morning's sunrise, every shifting wind, reminds us that meaning comes not from management but from trust.

2. Find joy in the ordinary

If life is vapor, then every breath is worth noticing. Qohelet's weariness with repetition calls us to rediscover wonder in what we often overlook: a shared meal, honest work, rest, love and friendship, laughter, beauty in nature. The Teacher will later tell us to eat, drink, and enjoy our toil as the gift of God—but that invitation begins here, in the ashes of false ambition. When we stop chasing the wind, we find grace in the simple. Joy is not a prize for the successful but a present for the grateful. Each ordinary moment becomes an act of worship when we receive it as gift rather than conquest.

3. Let wisdom lead to worship, not weariness

Qohelet warns that knowledge without reverence multiplies pain. The more we understand life's crookedness, the easier it is to become cynical. Yet wisdom's purpose is not to drain hope but to direct it upward. When we face the limits of our insight, we learn humility. When we admit that understanding can't fix everything, we learn to pray. True wisdom ends not in despair but in awe—recognizing that God's ways surpass ours and that our meaning rests in him, not in the endless chase "under the sun."

CONCLUSION

Qohelet's first reflections leave us unsettled but honest. The endless cycles of work, words, and wisdom expose how little control we possess. Yet this isn't despair—it's diagnosis. Before we can discover true joy, we must see the emptiness of every false pursuit. Life under the sun is vapor, but that very fragility invites reverence and gratitude.

Next, the Teacher turns from observation to experiment. In chapter 2, he tests every path we still chase—pleasure, achievement, wealth, wisdom—to see if any hold meaning. His journey will show that even success, stripped of God, leaves the same ache. The search continues, but the lesson deepens: everything matters only when seen as gift.

REFLECTION

1. What emotions surface when you hear that everything is "vanity" or vapor?
2. How does the phrase "under the sun" shape Qohelet's perspective on life?
3. What illusions of control do you most struggle to release?
4. Why do our words, eyes, and ears never seem satisfied?
5. How does the natural world mirror humanity's endless striving?
6. What does the burden of wisdom teach about humility and dependence on God?

DISCUSSION

1. How do modern people chase the wind in different ways than ancient ones?
2. Which parts of your daily routine feel most repetitive or unfulfilling?
3. What does it mean to find joy "under the sun" despite life's limits?
4. How can wisdom lead to worship instead of cynicism or despair?
5. What practices help you notice God's gifts in ordinary moments?
6. How might Ecclesiastes reshape the way we define success and satisfaction today?

2

WHEN SUCCESS ISN'T ENOUGH
ECCLESIASTES 2

Objective: To learn that achievement, pleasure, and wisdom cannot satisfy apart from God's presence and grace.

INTRODUCTION

A young executive once told a friend, "When I finally make partner, I'll rest." Five years later, with a corner office and six-figure bonus, he confessed, "Now I can't stop working." He was exhausted, successful, and restless—all at once. The problem wasn't laziness or greed; it was the illusion that satisfaction could be achieved through performance. His story could have been lifted straight from Ecclesiastes 2.

The Teacher begins this chapter by pursuing what most people only dream of: wealth, laughter, luxury, and legacy. He builds grand houses, plants vineyards, surrounds himself with art, music, and pleasure. He collects silver, gold, and the admiration of everyone around him. If anyone could prove that happiness comes from success, Qohelet would be the one. Yet when he finally stops to take it all in, the verdict is devastating: "Then I considered all that my hands had done… and behold, all was vanity and a chasing after wind."

Ecclesiastes 2 is one of the most honest chapters in the Bible about ambition and emptiness. It doesn't mock success; it unmasks it. The Teacher discovers that life's greatest joys cannot be engineered or earned. Meaning comes not from what we gather but from the God who gives. When success isn't enough, grace still is.

EXAMINATION

The pursuit of pleasure (2:1–3)

Qohelet begins chapter 2 by conducting the experiment he only announced in chapter 1. He moves from observation to participation: "I said in my heart, 'Come now, I will test you with pleasure; enjoy yourself.'" The Teacher steps into the life most people dream of—one without limits or restraint—to see if joy can be manufactured. Yet his opening verdict is immediate: "This also is vanity."

Pleasure, laughter, and wine represent three classic human escapes—entertainment, intoxication, and indulgence. The Teacher grants himself permission to explore them all, yet finds each hollow. "I said of laughter, 'It is mad,' and of pleasure, 'What use is it?'" The Hebrew word for "mad" means "foolish" or "irrational." Laughter distracts but cannot deliver. Wine may dull anxiety but cannot satisfy the heart. Qohelet admits he "guided his heart with wisdom," meaning he never lost himself entirely in recklessness. His goal was not hedonism but investigation: could controlled pleasure give meaning where wisdom failed?

The early answer is no. The momentary buzz of amusement fades into the same weary sigh. Qohelet's words echo every generation's search for "a good time" that lasts longer than a weekend. The Teacher's experiment ends where countless modern ones still do—with emptiness dressed as enjoyment.

Great projects and possessions (2:4–8)

When laughter and leisure fail, Qohelet tries legacy. "I made great works," he writes, "I built houses and planted vineyards for myself." The royal tone suggests Solomon's grandeur, yet the verbs throb with self-reference—"I made," "I built," "I gathered," "I acquired." His focus is entirely inward. The Teacher becomes both architect and audience of his own greatness.

He constructs gardens and parks, echoes of Eden recreated by human ambition. He amasses silver and gold, singers and servants, herds and concubines—every luxury available to an ancient monarch. The list reads like an inventory of success: art, nature, wealth, entertainment, sex. The dream is complete, yet the satisfaction still absent.

Qohelet's "great works" may remind readers of Israel's temple and palaces, yet the result is not glory but weariness. The impulse to build is divine—God created a garden, after all—but human building, detached from reverence, becomes a monument to self. The Teacher's possessions grow while his soul shrinks.

Modern readers see the same illusion: that productivity or prosperity will finally quiet the ache. We pour ourselves into houses, careers, projects, even ministries, believing the next accomplishment will make the difference. But like Qohelet, we discover that success multiplies the questions it cannot answer.

The experiment's result (2:9–11)

Qohelet summarizes the outcome of his royal experiment: "So I became great and surpassed all who were before me in Jerusalem." This is no failure of execution. He did everything right—wisdom guided him, wealth obeyed him, pleasure surrounded him. Yet the refrain returns: "Then I considered all that my hands had done… and behold, all was vanity and a chasing after wind."

His evaluation cuts to the heart of human striving. The problem is not the presence of pleasure but the absence of permanence. "There was nothing to be gained under the sun." The word *yitrôn* reappears—no lasting profit, no surplus. Achievement produces exhaustion rather than meaning. The Teacher has tasted every flavor of success, but none quench the thirst.

Qohelet's honesty disarms sentimentality. He does not condemn joy or work; he condemns their misuse as ultimate purpose. The house, the vineyard, the song, the silver—they are all good things that crumble under the weight of false expectation. He has everything and feels nothing.

Wisdom and folly compared (2:12–16)

The next phase of the Teacher's investigation shifts back to intellect. "Then I turned to consider wisdom and madness and folly." Having explored pleasure, he reexamines whether the mind can succeed where the senses failed. He concedes that wisdom is better than folly "as light is better than darkness." A wise person can see where he is going; a fool stumbles blindly. Wisdom improves life, just as light improves sight.

Yet even this advantage collapses before death. "The same event happens to all." Both the wise and the fool die, and both are soon forgotten. The Hebrew phrasing underscores futility—"Why then have I been so wise?" If wisdom cannot alter the final outcome, it offers no lasting advantage. The mind, like the body, meets the same end.

Qohelet's realism doesn't reject wisdom's value for daily life—it acknowledges its limit for ultimate meaning. Learning may guide us through time but cannot rescue us from it. Knowledge, no matter how vast, cannot conquer mortality. For all his brilliance, the Teacher still ends up in the same dust as the fool who never opened a book.

Hatred of toil (2:17–23)

The conclusion intensifies: "So I hated life." The Hebrew verb expresses not melodrama but deep revulsion—an emotional exhaustion with the treadmill of toil. "All is vanity and a chasing after wind." Work that once seemed noble now feels cruel. "For what has a man from all his toil and striving of heart with which he toils beneath the sun?"

Qohelet's despair sharpens around injustice: he must leave everything he built to someone who "did not toil for it." The Teacher foresees an heir who will enjoy what he never earned. "This also is vanity and a great evil." The bitterness reflects ancient royal anxiety about succession, yet its wisdom is timeless. We spend our lives accumulating wealth or wisdom, only to hand it off to those who may waste it.

He continues, "All his days are full of sorrow, and his work is vexation. Even in the night his heart does not rest." The image is haunting—success accompanied by insomnia. The very drive that built kingdoms now robs the Teacher of sleep. His achievements produce anxiety rather than peace. Work, stripped of trust in God, becomes an idol that demands sacrifice and never grants Sabbath.

Qohelet's words anticipate Jesus' warning centuries later: "What will it profit a man if he gains the whole world and forfeits his soul?" Every empire, business, or dream that ignores eternity eventually crushes its maker.

Finding grace in futility (2:24–26)

After pages of frustration, a surprising tone enters: "There is nothing better for a person than to eat and drink and find enjoyment in his toil." This refrain appears several times throughout the book and signals a turn toward grace. Qohelet is not reversing his earlier conclusions but reframing them. If everything under the sun is vapor, then meaning must come from above the sun—from God's gift, not human grasp.

"This also, I saw, is from the hand of God, for apart from him who can eat or who can have enjoyment?" The Teacher finds in simple pleasures a divine generosity that ambition never found. Food, drink, and work—mundane as they are—become sacraments of gratitude when received rather than seized.

To the one who pleases God, he says, God gives wisdom, knowledge, and joy. But to the sinner he gives the task of gathering and collecting, only to hand it over to the one who pleases God. This is poetic justice: the restless accumulate for the contented. Qohelet's contrast between the believer and the self-sufficient man reintroduces divine agency into his analysis. Human effort without reverence leads to frustration; human effort under God's hand yields contentment.

Qohelet does not yet command joy; he simply observes it as possibility. In a vapor-filled world, the only solid thing is God's grace. To eat, to drink, to work with gratitude—these are not futile acts but faithful ones. They do not defeat death, but they redeem the days leading to it.

The teacher's confession

Ecclesiastes 2 reads like a spiritual autobiography of success without satisfaction. The Teacher's experiment spans pleasure, projects, wisdom, and work, yet each ends in the same conclusion: none can secure meaning "under the sun." His reflections are not self-pitying but diagnostic. The problem is not enjoyment itself but autonomy—the attempt to wrest joy from creation without the Creator.

Qohelet's realism is a gift to Christians tempted by distraction or performance. He forces us to admit that busyness, wealth, and intellect cannot quiet the longing for eternity planted in our hearts. Meaning is not achieved; it is bestowed. Only when we stop treating life as a ladder to climb can we begin to receive it as table fellowship with God.

Chapter 2 thus prepares the way for the recurring theme of the entire book: joy is possible, but only as grace. The pursuit of success becomes the prelude to surrender. When success isn't enough, we finally learn that God is.

APPLICATION

1. Success without God always disappoints

Qohelet's pursuit of greatness sounds like the dream we all secretly chase: the perfect career, home, or reputation. Yet after achieving more than anyone before him, he confessed that it was all *hebel*—vapor. The tragedy was not in his failure but in his success. He gained everything except satisfaction. That warning still echoes for Christians today. We can do everything "right," yet if God is absent from the center, our joy evaporates. The human heart was not designed to be filled by accomplishment but by communion. The gospel exposes the same truth: what we achieve apart from God will never define us; what we receive from him always will. True fulfillment comes not from crossing finish lines, but from walking with the Lord who makes the journey meaningful.

2. Pleasure cannot heal the soul

Laughter, luxury, and leisure promise escape but deliver exhaustion. Qohelet discovered that pleasure divorced from purpose only amplifies emptiness. The more he indulged, the less satisfied he became. Pleasure is like salt water—it refreshes for a moment but increases thirst. Our culture often encourages endless amusement to drown anxiety, yet Ecclesiastes insists that distraction can't mend despair. The pursuit of fun without faith numbs pain but never cures it. Still, God isn't opposed to pleasure; he invented it. When received with gratitude, a meal, a song, or a sunset becomes worship. When seized without reverence, they become idols. The Christian's task is not to reject delight but to redeem it—to enjoy what God gives as gift rather than as god. Only then can joy deepen instead of disappear.

3. Work is a gift, not a god

Qohelet built palaces, vineyards, and parks—achievements that would have immortalized any ancient ruler. Yet all his toil left him sleepless and bitter. His hands were full, but his heart was empty. That tension remains familiar: the person who sacrifices rest, relationships, and righteousness on the altar of productivity soon discovers that work makes a terrible master. Labor was meant to reflect God's creativity, not replace his sovereignty. When our jobs define our worth, they become idols wearing business clothes. Ecclesiastes invites Christians to recover a theology of work: to labor diligently yet rest freely, to plan wisely yet trust humbly. Faith transforms our effort into offering; it releases us from the illusion that outcomes are ours to control. When we remember that God—not our performance—grants meaning, even ordinary tasks become sacred ground.

4. Contentment is the true reward

After exhausting every pursuit, the Teacher finally paused to eat, drink, and rejoice in simple blessings. This was not resignation but revelation. Joy, he realized, is not earned through conquest but received through contentment. In a world of endless comparison, Ecclesiastes whispers freedom: life's goodness is measured not by how much we accumulate but by how much we appreciate. Gratitude turns daily bread into feast, toil into worship, and companionship into grace. Contentment does not mean apathy toward improvement; it means serenity within limitation. We still plant, build, and dream—but without pretending those acts can save us. To "enjoy" in Qohelet's sense is to rest in the Giver's generosity. The content heart recognizes that every breath, every moment, every taste of joy is already a foretaste of eternity.

CONCLUSION

Qohelet's confession in chapter 2 feels uncomfortably modern. He had the laughter of parties, the applause of accomplishments, and the wealth of kings—yet none of it filled the silence of his soul. The problem was never the gifts themselves but the attempt to turn them into gods. Ecclesiastes pulls the curtain back on every human ambition and shows that joy is not the result of control but of communion.

Still, hope glimmers. The Teacher glimpses grace in eating, drinking, and enjoying what God provides. Meaning emerges not from escape but from gratitude. As we turn to chapter 3, the rhythm of time will take center stage: "For everything there is a season." There, Qohelet begins to show that wisdom finds peace not by conquering time but by trusting the One who rules over it.

REFLECTION

1. What emotions surface when success fails to satisfy?
2. Why is it easier to chase pleasure than to pursue peace?
3. How does Ecclesiastes expose the limits of achievement?
4. What role does gratitude play in genuine joy?
5. How do simple blessings reveal God's grace?
6. Why is contentment a greater victory than accomplishment?

DISCUSSION

1. What forms of "chasing the wind" tempt believers today?
2. How can Christians enjoy pleasure without letting it become idolatry?
3. In what ways can work become both gift and trap?
4. How does Ecclesiastes challenge our modern definitions of success?
5. What habits help us practice gratitude in daily life?
6. How can Christians model contentment in an anxious, achievement-driven world?

3

A SEASON FOR EVERYTHING

ECCLESIASTES 3

Objective: To learn to trust God's timing and find joy in life's appointed seasons.

INTRODUCTION

When farmers in ancient Israel looked to the heavens, they read the sky for timing. A season too early or too late could ruin an entire harvest. They could plow, plant, and pray—but only God could send the rain. Ecclesiastes 3 begins with that same humility: a recognition that time belongs to God. "There is a time for everything, and a season for every activity under heaven."

The Teacher's famous poem is more than poetic comfort; it is spiritual realism. Life is not random but rhythmic. Every birth, death, tear, and laugh unfolds within a divine pattern we seldom understand. Qohelet's list of opposites—gain and loss, war and peace—reminds us that we live between tensions we cannot control. The question is not whether seasons will change but how we will live within them.

For all its soberness, this passage radiates hope. God's hand is not only on the beginning and end but on every moment between. Ecclesiastes 3 invites believers to find peace in God's timing, gratitude in their portion, and joy in the fleeting beauty of the present. It teaches us that the secret to meaning is not escaping time but trusting the One who made it.

EXAMINATION

Time and eternity (3:1–8)

"There is a time for everything, and a season for every activity under the heavens." Few passages in Scripture are as lyrical or universally recognized as Qohelet's poem on time. It reads like a hymn of life—birth and death, weeping and laughter, war and peace. Fourteen pairs of opposites form a perfect symmetry, symbolizing completeness. Life's experiences move within boundaries we cannot control, yet each has its appointed moment.

Qohelet's tone is not sentimental. This is not a Hallmark meditation on balance; it is a sober reflection on limitation. The Hebrew term for "time" (*ēt*) carries the sense of a divinely appointed moment. God orders the flow of events, not humanity. Time is not a chaotic sequence but a pattern set by divine sovereignty. Humans act, choose, and feel—but within a framework not of their making.

The poem's rhythm mirrors the inevitability of life itself. The staccato repetitions—"a time to… a time to…"—sound like a clock ticking. The effect is both comforting and unsettling. Every joy has its shadow, every gain its loss. The Teacher forces us to admit what modern life tries hardest to deny: that time, not talent, rules the world.

Qohelet does not list moral opposites (good vs. evil) but experiential ones (birth vs. death, weeping vs. laughter). His concern is not ethics but existence. Both positive and negative moments belong in the fabric of reality. The one who plants will someday uproot; the one who embraces will someday refrain. Each action has its complement, suggesting that meaning lies not in any single experience but in recognizing God's governance over them all.

Human toil and divine timing (3:9–11)

After the poem, Qohelet returns to prose and his familiar question: "What gain has the worker from his toil?" The answer remains the same as before—none, at least not in the way humanity imagines. Yet here, the Teacher's tone softens. "He has made everything beautiful in its time." The word "beautiful" (*yāpeh*) may also mean "appropriate" or "fitting." What seems random to us is, in God's wisdom, timely.

Qohelet acknowledges that God's design possesses an elegance we cannot see. He adds, "He has also set eternity in their hearts, yet so that no one can find out what God has done from beginning to end." The paradox is profound. Humans long for more than the moment—they sense eternity—but they cannot grasp it. The capacity for transcendence collides with the boundary of finitude. We are creatures who know enough to ache for what we cannot comprehend.

This tension defines the human condition: we live in time but yearn for timelessness. The desire for permanence—through art, legacy, memory, or faith—reveals that eternity is written into our souls. Yet no amount of wisdom or effort can unravel the full tapestry of God's plan. The Creator's sovereignty remains beyond human calculation. Our task, then, is not to master time but to live faithfully within it.

The gift of joy (3:12–13)

Qohelet again turns from frustration to gratitude. "I perceived that there is nothing better for them than to be joyful and to do good as long as they live; also that everyone should eat and drink and take pleasure in all his toil—this is God's gift to man." The language echoes 2:24–25 but expands it. Human joy is not rebellion against life's futility but submission to divine generosity.

Here, "to do good" does not mean moral perfection but living well—acting with integrity, generosity, and gratitude in the brief time allotted. To "take pleasure" is not hedonism; it is acknowledgment that every small delight comes from God's hand. Ecclesiastes repeatedly returns to this refrain: while we cannot control time, we can sanctify the present by receiving it as grace.

Qohelet thus rejects both fatalism and frenzy. The fatalist shrugs that nothing matters; the frantic person insists that everything depends on their control. The Teacher offers a third path—joyful reverence. To eat, drink, and work with awareness of God's presence is to live wisely within the vapor.

The permanence of God's work (3:14–15)

"I perceived that whatever God does endures forever; nothing can be added to it, nor anything taken from it." This statement stands in contrast to the fleeting quality of human endeavor. Our work evaporates, but God's work remains. The phrase "God has done it so that people fear before him" introduces a central theme of the book's conclusion: reverence.

Qohelet's "fear" is not terror but awe—a recognition of divine sovereignty that humbles human pride. When we realize that our projects are temporary and God's purposes eternal, humility becomes worship. Verse 15 continues: "That which is, already has been; that which is to be, already has been; and God seeks what has been driven away." This cryptic phrase suggests that history is cyclical from the human view but purposeful in God's. Time may appear repetitive, yet nothing escapes divine attention. Even what seems lost, God "seeks again."

Qohelet does not deny God's involvement; he denies our capacity to map it. The eternal plan is not ours to edit. The comfort lies not in comprehension but in confidence: what God ordains endures.

Injustice and mortality (3:16–17)

After meditating on divine permanence, the Teacher turns back to earth: "Moreover, I saw under the sun that in the place of justice, even there was wickedness, and in the place of righteousness, even there was wickedness." Time may have order, but society does not. Courts meant for justice perpetuate corruption. Ecclesiastes refuses to idealize human systems.

Yet Qohelet responds not with nihilism but with faith: "God will judge the righteous and the wicked, for there is a time for every matter and for every work." The same God who orders seasons also governs moral history. Though injustice prevails temporarily, it will not endure forever. The Teacher's confidence in divine judgment may not erase present pain, but it anchors hope. Justice, like spring after winter, will have its season.

This conviction reaffirms the balance between realism and faith. Ecclesiastes never minimizes evil, yet it refuses to believe that evil has the last word. The God who controls times and seasons will also redeem them.

Humans and animals (3:18–21)

Qohelet then explores mortality with bracing candor. "I said in my heart with regard to the sons of men that God is testing them, that they may see that they themselves are but beasts." Death levels the playing field. "As one dies, so dies the other… all are from dust, and to dust all return."

This is not cynicism but humility. Humanity's physical fate mirrors that of animals—both breathe, both expire, both return to earth. Yet verse 21 introduces ambiguity: "Who knows whether the spirit of man goes upward and the spirit of the beast goes down into the earth?" The Hebrew construction suggests uncertainty, not denial. Qohelet refuses to claim knowledge beyond revelation. His question is rhetorical humility, not theological doubt.

The Teacher's point is ethical: mortality should humble pride. Awareness of death, properly understood, makes life more precious and gratitude more urgent. While he cannot articulate resurrection hope as later Scripture will, Qohelet recognizes that the boundary of death exposes the limits of human wisdom.

The call to contentment (3:22)

The chapter closes with a familiar refrain: "So I saw that there is nothing better than that a man should rejoice in his work, for that is his lot. Who can bring him to see what will be after him?" The Teacher accepts life as gift and limitation simultaneously. The phrase "that is his lot" recalls Israel's tribal inheritance—a portion given by God. Our "lot" is not punishment but provision: a finite share of time, task, and joy.

Qohelet's wisdom lies in embracing rather than escaping this portion. To rejoice in one's work does not mean blind optimism; it means grateful realism. We do not know what will come after us, but we can honor God with what is before us.

Ecclesiastes 3 thus resolves the tension of the earlier chapters without dissolving it. Life remains vapor, but God's presence makes even vapor radiant. Time remains uncontrollable, but it is not meaningless. The one who fears God learns to live rhythmically rather than anxiously—to inhabit time as grace instead of battle.

Living faithfully in time

Ecclesiastes 3 invites Christians to surrender control without surrendering purpose. The Teacher's poem reminds us that every event in life—birth and death, mourning and dancing—falls within divine appointment. God's sovereignty over time does not erase human responsibility; it sanctifies it. Our task is to live fully in each appointed season, trusting that God makes everything fitting in its time.

Qohelet's vision blends realism and reverence. The clock keeps ticking, the graves keep filling, yet God's work endures forever. The wise learn not to fight time but to fellowship with the One who stands outside it. When we live with eternity in our hearts and gratitude in our hands, we discover that even fleeting moments can carry eternal weight.

APPLICATION

1. Trust God's timing when life feels out of season

Ecclesiastes 3 teaches that God's sovereignty extends over every human experience. There is "a time to weep and a time to laugh," but we rarely know which is which until afterward. Our impatience insists that every pain end now, yet the Teacher calls us to faith: God makes everything beautiful—or fitting—in its time. Trusting his timing does not mean understanding it. It means believing that his hand is steady even when the calendar feels cruel. The Christian who accepts God's seasons learns to stop forcing outcomes and start walking by faith. The same God who governs the sunrise governs your sorrow. Waiting becomes worship when we believe that no season is wasted in his purpose.

2. Live with eternity in your heart, not anxiety in your mind

Qohelet says God has "set eternity in the human heart," yet we cannot grasp what he is doing from beginning to end. That tension defines faith. We are built for forever but confined to now. The temptation is to fill that gap with worry or ambition, trying to control what lies beyond our reach. Instead, Ecclesiastes invites us to rest in mystery. To live with eternity in our hearts means to see today as sacred, not insignificant. It means we treat every conversation, task, and breath as part of a story larger than our lifespan. Eternity does not make the present meaningless; it makes it weighty. The wise do not demand answers—they practice presence.

3. Practice joy as an act of faith

Qohelet insists that joy itself is a gift: to eat, drink, and find pleasure in one's toil is from God's hand. Joy is not denial of life's brevity but defiance against despair. In a world obsessed with productivity, choosing gratitude is spiritual rebellion. When we enjoy a meal, conversation, or quiet moment of rest, we confess that the Creator still reigns. Biblical joy is not an emotional high but a theological stance—a declaration that even fleeting goodness is evidence of divine generosity. The Teacher's wisdom reminds us that contentment is not achieved; it is received. Each day offers a chance to practice joy, to thank God for the portion he provides, and to trust him for what remains unseen.

4. Let reverence replace control

Qohelet concludes that "whatever God does endures forever." Our projects fade, our schedules crumble, our plans unravel—but God's work stands firm. The only proper response is reverence. To "fear God" in Ecclesiastes means to live with awe, humility, and surrender. It means giving up the illusion that we can add or subtract from divine wisdom. The one who fears God can finally rest, because the outcome no longer depends on their grasp. Reverence transforms anxiety into peace and effort into worship. Every season—gain and loss, joy and grief—becomes an altar where trust is renewed. To fear God is not to cower before mystery but to bow in gratitude before majesty. In that posture, life's rhythm becomes music instead of noise.

CONCLUSION

Qohelet's poem on time is both comfort and confrontation. It comforts us with the assurance that God orders the flow of life; it confronts us with the truth that we do not. Every gain and loss, laughter and tear, stands within his plan. The wise heart stops fighting time and starts trusting God's rhythm.

As the book continues, the Teacher will turn from the order of time to the disorder of society. In chapter 4, he surveys oppression, isolation, and rivalry—reminding us that even when life feels unjust, God still calls us to community and compassion. Seasons change, but the call to faithfulness remains. In every time and every task, our joy is still God's gift.

REFLECTION

1. What emotions arise when you consider that every event has its appointed time?
2. How does Ecclesiastes 3 challenge your view of control and planning?
3. Why is it difficult to trust God's timing in painful seasons?
4. What does it mean to live with eternity in your heart?
5. How can joy function as an act of faith?
6. What helps you replace anxiety with reverence in daily life?

DISCUSSION

1. Which pair in 3:1–8 most resonates with your current season?
2. How do you see God's order in the apparent chaos of the world?
3. What practices help you cultivate gratitude in ordinary routines?
4. In what ways can Christians model peace in an anxious culture?
5. How does belief in God's eternal work shape our approach to injustice?
6. What does it mean to "rejoice in your work" as your God-given lot?

4

BETTER TOGETHER (AND SOMETIMES NOT)

ECCLESIASTES 4

Objective: To recognize that companionship reflects God's design and protects against the vanity of self-sufficiency.

INTRODUCTION

In 1960, a group of mountaineers attempted to climb the Eiger in the Swiss Alps. Midway up the icy wall, one man slipped. The rope stretched taut, catching him—but only because it was tied to the others. "If I had been climbing alone," he said later, "I would have died." His words echo the wisdom of Ecclesiastes 4: "Two are better than one."

Qohelet's reflections in this chapter expose both the pain of isolation and the power of companionship. He sees oppression crushing the powerless, competition fueling endless rivalry, and loneliness haunting the successful. But he also sees hope in partnership—friends who lift one another, share warmth, and face hardship side by side. At the same time, he warns that not all togetherness brings meaning: even leadership and popularity fade into vapor.

Ecclesiastes 4 reminds us that we were created for community, not competition. We are better together—but only when our relationships rest on humility, not pride; on service, not self. The Teacher's wisdom urges Christians to value people over possessions, compassion over control, and faithfulness over fame.

EXAMINATION

Oppression under the sun (4:1–3)

Qohelet opens this section with one of the most haunting observations in Scripture: "Again I saw all the oppressions that are done under the sun." The adverb "again" connects this reflection to the injustice of 3:16–17 but takes the lament further. Here, the Teacher no longer speaks abstractly of courts and systems but personally of victims—people crushed beneath power without comfort or advocate. He sees "the tears of the oppressed, and they had no one to comfort them."

This vision is raw and unfiltered. The repetition of "no comforter" echoes like a funeral toll. The Teacher's empathy extends beyond statistics to shared sorrow. Unlike other wisdom texts that uphold order and reward, Ecclesiastes stares into disorder and pain. The reality is not what theology expects: the wicked thrive, and the righteous suffer.

Qohelet concludes that "on the side of their oppressors there was power." Power, not justice, shapes life under the sun. In that despair, he voices an unthinkable thought: "I declared that the dead, who have already died, are happier than the living who are still alive. But better than both is he who has not yet been, who has not seen the evil done under the sun." This is not a suicidal wish but an existential lament. It is the sigh of one who feels the weight of unrighted wrongs.

His words echo Job's cry (Job 3:11–19) and Israel's exilic grief. Ecclesiastes acknowledges that even faith must sometimes speak from darkness. In a world marred by injustice, Qohelet dares to name sorrow without explaining it away. Faith that cannot lament is too fragile for real life.

Rivalry and restless ambition (4:4–6)

The Teacher moves from social oppression to personal competition: "Then I saw that all toil and all skill in work come from a person's envy of another. This also is vanity and a chasing after wind." What begins as creative energy often ends as comparison. Human achievement, he observes, frequently grows from rivalry, not virtue. The craftsman's excellence or the scholar's diligence may stem not from joy in the task but jealousy of another's success.

Qohelet does not condemn labor itself but the motive behind it. Work fueled by envy can never rest; it feeds on perpetual dissatisfaction. The "chasing after wind" returns as the image of endless motion without arrival. To live for competition is to live enslaved to someone else's shadow.

Then comes a proverb contrasting laziness and overwork: "The fool folds his hands and consumes his own flesh. Better is a handful of quietness than two handfuls of toil and a chasing after wind." The fool's idleness devours him; the workaholic's striving depletes him. Wisdom lies in the middle path—a handful of rest, a contented heart. The Hebrew word for "quietness" (*năhat*) conveys not apathy but tranquility, the peace that comes from enough.

In these verses, Ecclesiastes critiques both extremes of human behavior. The lazy waste their lives through inaction; the ambitious waste them through excess. Between the two lies wisdom: the satisfaction that comes from labor done in gratitude, not rivalry.

The tragedy of isolation (4:7–8)

"Again, I saw vanity under the sun: one person who has no other, either son or brother, yet there is no end to all his toil." Qohelet paints the portrait of the lonely laborer—successful, wealthy, and utterly alone. The image is striking: a man driven to accumulate more though no one shares in his gain. "His eyes are never satisfied with riches, and he never asks, 'For whom am I toiling?'"

This vignette cuts to the heart of modern culture. Ambition isolates. The man's endless work has cost him community. He is trapped in self-made solitude, mistaking wealth for purpose. The Teacher calls this condition "vanity and an unhappy business." The phrase may also mean "a grievous task"—a life that produces everything except joy.

Qohelet exposes the spiritual poverty beneath material success. Without relationship, achievement becomes hollow. The human heart was created for fellowship—both with others and with God. When life is defined by output rather than connection, loneliness becomes the ultimate consequence of idolatry.

The blessing of companionship (4:9–12)

From the tragedy of isolation, the Teacher turns to the wisdom of relationship: "Two are better than one, because they have a good reward for their toil." Companionship, unlike competition, multiplies joy. Partnership transforms labor from burden to blessing.

Qohelet lists three benefits of community. First, *mutual help*: "If they fall, one will lift up his companion." Ancient travelers risked injury on rocky paths; to walk alone was to court disaster. Second, *warmth*: "If two lie together, they keep warm." In a cold, arid climate, shared body heat could mean survival. Third, *protection*: "Though one may be overpowered, two can defend themselves." Companionship provides safety against both circumstance and enemy.

The concluding proverb—"A threefold cord is not quickly broken"—expands the principle. Whether it refers to friendship, marriage, or communal life, the point stands: strength increases with solidarity. In a world filled with injustice and competition, partnership becomes an act of resistance.

Qohelet's vision of companionship anticipates the New Testament's teaching that Christians form one body. Yet his tone remains realistic: relationships are not perfect solutions but precious supports. Shared burdens do not remove life's vapor; they simply make it bearable.

The vanity of popularity (4:13–16)

The final section of the chapter introduces a brief parable about political success and its short lifespan. "Better is a poor but wise youth than an old but foolish king who no longer knows how to take advice." The story contrasts humility with pride. Wisdom, not wealth or age, defines true greatness. The young man rises "from prison to the throne," while the old king declines through arrogance.

At first, the youth's ascent seems hopeful. "There was no end of all the people whom he led." Yet the admiration of the crowd soon fades: "Those who come later will not rejoice in him." Popularity proves as vaporous as pleasure or power. Every generation forgets its heroes.

This brief narrative echoes the cycles already described in chapter 3. Time erases fame as surely as death erases memory. The story may recall Joseph's rise from prison or Israel's revolving kings, but its meaning transcends history: leadership without humility ends in futility. The applause of the crowd lasts only until the next youth replaces the last.

Qohelet's point is subtle but devastating. Not even community guarantees meaning if it becomes a platform for pride. The lonely man of verses 7-8 worked for himself; the ambitious ruler of verses 13–16 works for applause. Both end the same way—alone.

Life's need for relationship and reverence

Ecclesiastes 4 is the Teacher's exploration of how human relationships—social, personal, and political—can both relieve and reveal vanity. Oppression shows the cruelty of power without compassion; rivalry exposes the emptiness of ambition without rest; isolation uncovers the pain of success without companionship; and unstable leadership reveals the folly of influence without humility.

Through it all, Qohelet hints at what humanity truly needs: not control but connection, not applause but empathy. The remedy to vanity is not withdrawal from others but wise engagement with them. Life "under the sun" remains vapor, yet the shared warmth of friendship and the humble fear of God give it shape and dignity.

Injustice and ambition will always haunt human existence, but Ecclesiastes insists that relationships grounded in humility can still reflect divine goodness. When two walk together in faith, their steps may not escape the wind—but they no longer chase it alone.

APPLICATION

1. Stand with the oppressed

Qohelet's first cry is not philosophical but compassionate. "I saw the tears of the oppressed, and they had no comforter." Faith begins not by explaining suffering but by standing beside it. The Teacher's grief exposes a truth often forgotten in comfortable religion: God's people are called to be comforters in a comfortless world. We cannot fix every injustice, but we can refuse to look away. When power crushes the powerless, silence becomes complicity. Ecclesiastes challenges us to embody mercy—to listen, to defend, to lift the fallen. The Christian response to oppression is not detachment but empathy. To weep with those who weep (Rom. 12:15) is itself an act of worship, declaring that life matters because the Creator values every soul. Compassion may not solve vanity, but it redeems it through love.

2. Learn the quiet joy of enough

Between the lazy fool and the driven workaholic lies a rare and sacred word: *enough*. Qohelet calls it "a handful of quietness." It is the wisdom of contentment—a life not wasted by apathy or consumed by ambition. A large segment of our culture glorifies hustle and condemns rest, yet Ecclesiastes reminds us that relentless striving is also vanity. The wise learn to labor faithfully without letting work define their worth. When we seek contentment instead of comparison, rest becomes worship and simplicity becomes strength. *Enough* does not mean mediocrity; it means freedom. It is the ability to stop chasing the wind because we trust that God's portion is sufficient. The one who learns to rest in God's provision finds more satisfaction in one handful of grace than in two handfuls of exhaustion.

3. Cherish community as God's gift

"Two are better than one," Qohelet writes, and every believer knows why. Companionship turns toil into teamwork and sorrow into solace. We were never designed for isolation. Friendship is more than convenience—it is divine provision. Yet genuine community requires humility. We must be willing both to lift and to be lifted, to warm and to be warmed. Ecclesiastes 4 portrays relationships as sacred survival: one falls, the other helps him rise; one shivers, the other shares warmth; one faces danger, the other defends. The "threefold cord" may symbolize marriage, friendship, or fellowship among Christian—any bond woven by faith and love. In a world driven by self-promotion, godly relationships remind us that meaning grows through mutual care. Alone, we crumble; together, we endure.

4. Pursue humility over popularity

Qohelet's parable of the poor youth and the old king exposes a timeless temptation: the hunger for recognition. The young leader rises, the crowd cheers, and soon the applause fades. Every generation forgets its heroes. Ecclesiastes reminds us that fame is a fragile currency—it cannot purchase peace. The wise learn that influence without humility becomes vanity. The better goal is not being celebrated but being faithful. Leadership, whether in the church, the home, or the workplace, should serve others rather than seek applause. God values character more than charisma, endurance more than popularity. The old king's folly was pride; the young ruler's tragedy was being forgotten. Both warn us that human praise evaporates quickly, but God's approval endures. The humble heart finds security not in being remembered, but in being known by God.

CONCLUSION

Qohelet's vision of life under the sun moves from the loneliness of oppression to the warmth of fellowship. We were not made to walk alone. Companionship cannot remove life's vapor, but it can make the journey bearable. True success is measured not by what we build, but by whom we bless along the way.

Yet the Teacher ends with a warning: even shared glory can turn to pride. The crowds that cheer today may forget tomorrow. Chapter 5 will turn from human relationships to our relationship with God—calling us to approach him with reverence and humility. Before we speak many words or chase many dreams, Ecclesiastes reminds us: worship begins with listening.

REFLECTION

1. How does Ecclesiastes 4 challenge your view of success and independence?
2. Where do you see modern forms of oppression or injustice around you?
3. What does "a handful of quietness" look like in your life?
4. Why is companionship necessary for enduring hardship?
5. How can humility protect Christians from the vanity of popularity?
6. What relationships help you stay grounded in faith and gratitude?

DISCUSSION

1. What emotions arise when Qohelet says the dead are happier than the living?
2. How do ambition and comparison rob us of contentment?
3. What makes building authentic community difficult in today's culture?
4. How can churches embody the "two are better than one" principle?
5. What lessons about leadership emerge from the parable of the old king?
6. How can Christians use power or influence without falling into vanity?

5

GUARD YOUR STEPS

ECCLESIASTES 5

Objective: To approach God with reverence and receive life's blessings with gratitude and humility.

INTRODUCTION

A tourist once visited a monastery known for its vow of silence. During lunch, the monks ate quietly until one stood and said, "The soup is cold." A year later, another monk rose and replied, "It was warm last year." After another long pause, the abbot sighed, "If you two don't stop arguing, you'll ruin the peace." The humor hides a truth Qohelet understood well—silence before God is wiser than many words.

In Ecclesiastes 5, the Teacher walks us into the temple and warns, "Guard your steps when you go to the house of God." After exposing the vanity of ambition and injustice, he turns to the vanity of careless worship. Empty words, rash vows, and restless greed all dishonor the God who gives life. True faith, he says, begins with awe and ends with gratitude.

This chapter moves from the sanctuary to the marketplace, from vows to wealth, showing that reverence must govern every part of life. God is not impressed by our noise or possessions but pleased by our humility and thankfulness. When we learn to approach him with quiet hearts and open hands, worship becomes the cure for both greed and fear.

EXAMINATION

Approaching God with reverence (5:1–3)

Qohelet turns from social relationships to sacred ones. After observing human injustice and vanity, he now addresses the temple—where people meet God. "Guard your steps when you go to the house of God." The Hebrew phrase literally means "watch your feet," a metaphor for mindfulness. Worship is not casual. To come before the Almighty is to enter holy space, not a marketplace for words or deals.

Qohelet contrasts two kinds of worshipers: the listener and the talker. "Draw near to listen rather than to offer the sacrifice of fools, for they do not know that they are doing evil." The "sacrifice of fools" may refer to thoughtless rituals or empty offerings—acts of devotion performed without obedience. In Israel's wisdom tradition, listening is the truest form of worship because it acknowledges God's sovereignty. The fool substitutes noise for reverence, busyness for obedience.

The Teacher cautions, "Do not be rash with your mouth, nor let your heart be hasty to utter a word before God." True piety requires silence, not verbosity. God is in heaven, we are on earth; the distance between Creator and creature demands humility. "Therefore let your words be few." Like Job at the end of his ordeal, Qohelet knows that awe—not argument—is the proper response to divine majesty.

"Dreams come with much business, and a fool's voice with many words." The proverb suggests that just as an overworked mind breeds restless dreams, an unrestrained tongue breeds folly. Worship should quiet, not inflate, the self. Reverence begins when the noise of ambition fades into attentive stillness.

Keeping vows and speaking truth (5:4–7)

Qohelet now warns against making promises to God lightly: "When you vow a vow to God, do not delay in paying it, for he has no pleasure in fools. Pay what you vow." In the ancient world, vows were voluntary but binding. A person might promise a gift or offering if God granted help in distress. But once uttered, the vow became sacred obligation. To delay fulfillment was to mock God's holiness and faithfulness.

"It is better that you should not vow than that you should vow and not pay." This counsel echoes Deuteronomy 23:21–23 and Proverbs 20:25. God does not need vows; humans make them out of desperation or pride. Qohelet's wisdom is practical and theological: our words reveal our integrity. To use God's name as leverage or insurance cheapens worship.

He adds, "Let not your mouth lead you into sin, and do not say before the messenger that it was a mistake." The "messenger" may refer to a temple official responsible for verifying vows. Qohelet warns against backpedaling—claiming the vow was an error to escape responsibility. "Why should God be angry at your voice and destroy the work of your hands?" Even ritual deceit carries consequence.

"For when dreams increase and words grow many, there is vanity; but God is the one you must fear." The repetition of "dreams" and "many words" links back to verse 3. Human imagination often multiplies promises it cannot keep. True wisdom remembers the hierarchy: God reigns in heaven; humans speak from dust. The remedy for empty religion is not more emotion but more awe.

Oppression and bureaucracy (5:8–9)

Without warning, Qohelet returns to political observation: "If you see in a province the oppression of the poor and the violation of justice and righteousness, do not be astonished at the matter." His shift from worship to injustice may seem abrupt, but the link is moral: reverence for God should produce righteousness toward others. When worship loses integrity, society follows.

Qohelet describes a bureaucratic hierarchy of exploitation—officials watching officials, each protecting their own advantage. "The high official is watched by a higher one, and there are yet higher ones over them." The image anticipates the corruption of empire and the frustration of ordinary people. Yet he tempers the critique with a proverb: "But this is gain for a land in every way: a king committed to cultivated fields." Some interpreters read this as sarcasm—Qohelet's way of saying even kings serve self-interest; others see it as a concession that stability is better than chaos. Either way, the Teacher acknowledges that injustice is embedded in every human system.

The transition from the temple to the marketplace reminds readers that piety without justice is hypocrisy. God is not fooled by eloquent prayers offered by those who exploit others. True worship shows itself in honest living.

The futility of wealth (5:10–12)

"Whoever loves money will not be satisfied with money, nor he who loves abundance with gain." Qohelet's critique of greed continues the theme of *hebel*—the vaporous pursuit of satisfaction through accumulation. Desire, once indulged, only multiplies. The appetite for wealth expands faster than wealth itself.

"When goods increase, they increase who eat them, and what advantage has their owner but to see them with his eyes?" Prosperity attracts dependents, taxes, and thieves; the more one gains, the less one keeps. Wealth brings attention, not peace. In contrast, "the sleep of a laborer is sweet, whether he eats little or much, but the abundance of the rich will not let him sleep." Simplicity produces rest; affluence produces anxiety.

Qohelet exposes the irony of human ambition. The poor man, though limited, sleeps soundly; the rich man, though secure, lies awake calculating his risk. Wealth promises freedom but delivers bondage. As in previous chapters, the Teacher doesn't condemn possessions—he condemns their tyranny. The true enemy of joy is not poverty but preoccupation.

The tragedy of hoarded riches (5:13–17)

"There is a grievous evil that I have seen under the sun: riches were kept by their owner to his hurt." The hoarder, fearful of loss, becomes enslaved to his possessions. His wealth vanishes through misfortune, leaving him nothing for his children. The story illustrates the fragility of fortune and the folly of misplaced trust.

"As he came from his mother's womb, he shall go again, naked as he came." Death renders wealth irrelevant. Like Job, Qohelet reminds us that we depart with as little as we arrived. "He takes nothing for his toil that he may carry away in his hand." Human striving, detached from reverence, ends in empty hands.

The Teacher calls this "a grievous evil"—not only because it is unfair, but because it is inevitable. The pursuit of gain under the sun concludes in darkness: "All his days he eats in darkness, with much vexation and sickness and anger." The image portrays the miser at his lonely table, surrounded by abundance yet starved of joy (Ebenezer Scrooge). Greed, not deprivation, is the true poverty.

Receiving joy as God's gift (5:18–20)

Qohelet concludes the section with a radiant counterpoint to the gloom: "Behold, what I have seen to be good and fitting is to eat and drink and find enjoyment in all the toil with which one toils under the sun the few days of his life that God has given him." This is the Teacher's refrain of grace. In a world ruled by injustice and instability, joy survives as a divine gift.

"Everyone also to whom God has given wealth and possessions and power to enjoy them, and to accept his lot and rejoice in his toil—this is the gift of God." The ability to enjoy is as miraculous as the gift itself. Many have wealth; few have contentment. Enjoyment, therefore, is not indulgence but thanksgiving.

"For he will not much remember the days of his life because God keeps him occupied with joy in his heart." The phrase "not remember" does not imply forgetfulness but freedom—liberation from the anxious self-consciousness that plagues those obsessed with gain. God grants such joy that life's brevity no longer feels like futility.

Qohelet's theology here is subtle but revolutionary: meaning is not achieved through striving but received through trust. The Teacher does not abolish the vapor; he teaches us to live faithfully within it. To "fear God" (5:7) and to "enjoy God's gifts" (5:19) are not opposites but partners. Reverence guards joy from arrogance; gratitude guards reverence from despair.

Worship, wealth, and wisdom

Ecclesiastes 5 unites two realms often separated—worship and work. The Teacher moves from the temple to the treasury, exposing vanity in both religion and economics. In worship, vanity appears as empty words and broken vows; in wealth, it appears as restless accumulation and joyless abundance. The cure for both is the same: *fear God and receive what he gives.*

Qohelet's realism invites Christians to a life of simplicity and sincerity. True reverence listens before it speaks, acts before it boasts, and gives before it grasps. The wise worshiper knows that God is not impressed by volume but by humility. The wise worker knows that money cannot buy rest or joy.

In a noisy world full of promises and pursuits, Ecclesiastes 5 whispers ancient counsel still needed today: guard your steps, keep your vows, enjoy your portion, and remember that everything beautiful "under the sun" is sustained by the God who reigns above it.

APPLICATION

1. Approach worship with awe, not routine

Qohelet's first command—"Guard your steps when you go to the house of God"—reminds us that reverence begins long before the first song or prayer. Worship is not performance but presence. In a culture that treats the sacred as casual, Ecclesiastes calls believers to recover holy attentiveness. To "draw near to listen" means to come ready to hear, not to impress. God desires hearts that tremble, not tongues that boast. Worship stripped of humility becomes noise. The cure for empty religion is not louder praise but deeper silence. When we enter God's presence with awe, our words slow down and our spirits open up. The wise worshiper remembers who is in heaven and who is on earth—and that grace, not eloquence, is what keeps us standing there.

2. Keep your promises before God and people

In Qohelet's day, vows were voluntary yet sacred; in ours, they are frequent yet forgotten. Whether in marriage, ministry, or daily speech, our promises still matter. Ecclesiastes warns against using God's name to polish our image or to make bargains we won't honor. Integrity is the foundation of faith. When words outpace obedience, worship loses credibility. "Better not to vow than to vow and not pay." Faithfulness in speech is one of the clearest proofs of reverence. Every unkept promise erodes trust—both human and divine. Jesus echoed this same wisdom: "Let your 'Yes' be yes and your 'No,' no" (Matt. 5:37). God delights in quiet honesty more than dramatic pledges.

3. Pursue simplicity instead of striving

Ecclesiastes exposes the emptiness of both greed and anxiety. "Whoever loves money will not be satisfied with money." The lesson is timeless: possessions expand our pressure more than our peace. The richer the person, the more restless the soul—unless gratitude intervenes. Qohelet's comparison between the rich man's sleeplessness and the laborer's rest invites us to rediscover contentment. Satisfaction does not come from abundance but acceptance. When we learn to enjoy our portion as gift, rather than proof of success, work becomes worship. Simplicity is not poverty—it is freedom from preoccupation. The Christian's peace lies in stewardship, not ownership. The hands that cling to less can hold joy more securely. To love God above gold is to rest in the quiet confidence that we already have enough.

4. Receive joy as a sacred gift

"Everyone to whom God has given wealth and the power to enjoy it… this is the gift of God." The Teacher reminds us that joy is not earned through wisdom, work, or wealth—it is bestowed. The greatest miracle is not possession but perception: the ability to see blessings as blessings. When we recognize life's pleasures as undeserved gifts, even simple meals and daily tasks become holy. The believer's joy is not denial of pain but trust in providence. God "keeps him occupied with joy in his heart," freeing him from anxious self-focus. Worship that begins in reverence ends in rejoicing. The one who fears God the most enjoys life the best, because gratitude has turned every moment—bright or dim—into evidence of divine grace.

CONCLUSION

Ecclesiastes 5 teaches that the difference between vanity and meaning lies in reverence. Foolish worship multiplies words; faithful worship multiplies wonder. The same God who rules heaven also gives joy on earth, turning ordinary labor into holy gratitude. Qohelet's wisdom reminds us that worship and work are never separate—both are acts of trust.

As the next chapter unfolds, the Teacher will turn again to the riddle of wealth and dissatisfaction. Chapter 6 exposes how prosperity without gratitude becomes punishment. But the invitation remains unchanged: to live humbly before God, to enjoy the portion he provides, and to remember that every good thing is gift.

REFLECTION

1. Why does Qohelet warn us to "guard our steps" in worship?
2. How can reverence protect us from empty religion?
3. What does it mean to let our words be few before God?
4. Why do unkept promises damage both faith and community?
5. How does wealth often steal rather than supply contentment?
6. What helps you enjoy life's simple gifts with gratitude?

DISCUSSION

1. What emotions arise when you imagine standing before God in silence?
2. How can modern worship sometimes resemble the "sacrifice of fools"?
3. What habits can help us honor our vows to God and others?
4. Why is contentment harder to learn in a culture of abundance?
5. How do gratitude and humility work together to produce joy?
6. What does it look like to receive wealth as stewardship, not status?

6

THE UNFULFILLED LIFE
ECCLESIASTES 6

Objective: To realize that joy comes from gratitude to God, not from gain, longevity, or understanding.

INTRODUCTION

In 1923, seven of the world's most powerful businessmen met at Chicago's Edgewater Beach Hotel. They controlled more money than the U.S. Treasury and were hailed as "masters of the economy." Twenty-five years later, most were bankrupt, imprisoned, or dead by suicide. They had conquered the world—and lost their souls.

Ecclesiastes 6 reads like a commentary on that tragedy. The Teacher describes a man who has wealth, possessions, and honor, yet lacks "the power to enjoy them." A stranger consumes what he cannot. Life, for all its riches, becomes a hollow performance. Qohelet calls this "a grievous evil," not because the man sinned more than others, but because he mistook abundance for blessing.

Here, the Teacher exposes a truth that time cannot erode: joy is not acquired but given. The ability to enjoy life's good gifts is divine grace, not human achievement. Ecclesiastes 6 warns us that desire, ungoverned by gratitude, breeds despair. The unfulfilled life is not the poor life—it is the one that cannot rest in God's goodness.

EXAMINATION

The problem of prosperity without joy (6:1–2)

Qohelet begins with an arresting observation: "There is an evil that I have seen under the sun, and it lies heavy on mankind." The word "evil" (*ra'*) here describes not moral wickedness but a grievous misfortune—a distortion in the moral fabric of life. What he describes next strikes at the heart of human desire: "A man to whom God gives wealth, possessions, and honor, so that he lacks nothing of all that he desires, yet God does not give him power to enjoy them, but a stranger enjoys them."

This is one of Ecclesiastes' most painful paradoxes. The man has everything except the capacity for contentment. The Teacher's realism cuts deep: satisfaction is not a product of possessions but a gift from God. The "power to enjoy" is divine, not human, and cannot be purchased or planned. To have abundance without gratitude is, in Qohelet's words, "vanity—it is a grievous evil."

The image of the "stranger" enjoying what the rich man cannot heightens the tragedy. Whether it refers to an heir, an adversary, or a foreign invader, the point stands: joy cannot be inherited or outsourced. Without the grace of enjoyment, even wealth becomes judgment.

A thousand years without joy (6:3–6)

Qohelet presses the argument with stark imagery: "If a man fathers a hundred children and lives many years, so that the days of his years are many, but his soul is not satisfied with life's good things, and he also has no burial, I say that a stillborn child is better off than he."

The Teacher exaggerates deliberately to expose vanity's depth. In ancient Israel, long life, many children, and honorable burial were considered the ultimate signs of divine blessing. Yet here, the man who has them all finds no rest. The stillborn child, by contrast, escapes the struggle. "It comes in vanity and goes in darkness, and in darkness its name is covered." The brevity of the infant's existence spares it from the pain of dissatisfaction.

Qohelet's comparison is not callous but contemplative. He does not diminish the grief of loss but uses it to expose the emptiness of a joyless existence. "Even though he should live a thousand years twice over, yet enjoy no good—do not all go to the one place?" Death equalizes all achievements. Without contentment, even long life becomes long misery.

The passage anticipates later biblical wisdom: abundance without thankfulness is a curse. True blessing is not measured in years or offspring but in the ability to see good in what God gives.

The insatiable appetite of the soul (6:7–9)

"All the toil of man is for his mouth, yet his appetite is not satisfied." With this proverb, Qohelet shifts from external wealth to internal hunger. The "mouth" represents human need; the "appetite" (*nephesh*, or "soul") represents desire. Labor sustains life but never fulfills it. We eat to live, yet living only deepens hunger.

The Teacher observes that neither the wise nor the fool escapes this cycle: "For what advantage has the wise man over the fool? And what does the poor man have who knows how to conduct himself before the living?" Knowledge and prudence may improve circumstance but cannot satisfy the soul. The hunger of the heart outlasts every meal.

Qohelet concludes with another proverb: "Better is the sight of the eyes than the wandering of the appetite." This echoes the biblical ideal of contentment. The "sight of the eyes" means enjoying what is before you; the "wandering of the appetite" means restless craving for what is not. Gratitude anchors the heart; desire drives it mad.

"This also is vanity and a chasing after wind." The Teacher's realism warns against endless striving disguised as self-improvement. Our age still lives by the same illusion—that satisfaction is just one upgrade away. Ecclesiastes punctures that fantasy with ancient precision: longing, unbridled, becomes its own prison.

The limits of human power and knowledge (6:10–12)

"What has come to be has already been named, and it is known what man is, and that he is not able to dispute with one stronger than he." The Teacher closes the section with a meditation on limitation. Humanity's boundaries—set by creation itself—cannot be argued away. The word "named" recalls Genesis, where naming signified dominion. To say that everything "has already been named" is to confess that God's sovereignty extends over all events. We may strive, but we do not define.

"The more words, the more vanity, and what is the advantage to man?" Eloquence cannot erase reality. Philosophical debate, political rhetoric, even religious talk—all collapse before the mystery of providence. The one who "disputes with one stronger" is the person who resents divine sovereignty, demanding explanations that God withholds.

Qohelet ends with two rhetorical questions: "For who knows what is good for man while he lives the few days of his vain life, which he passes like a shadow? For who can tell man what will be after him under the sun?" Both emphasize ignorance. We cannot know what is truly best, nor can we predict what comes next. Life's brevity and uncertainty force humility.

The word "shadow" evokes Psalm 144:4: "Man is like a breath; his days are like a passing shadow." Human existence is fleeting and opaque. We live between desire and death, ignorance and faith. The Teacher does not mock this condition; he dignifies it by honesty. To recognize our limits is not despair but wisdom.

The poverty of plenty

Ecclesiastes 6 completes a two-chapter reflection on wealth and satisfaction. In chapter 5, Qohelet showed that enjoyment is God's gift; in chapter 6, he shows that without that gift, prosperity becomes punishment. The man with abundance but without gratitude lives a shorter, darker life than the child who never saw the sun.

The chapter's closing verses frame humanity's ultimate dilemma: we are creatures of appetite living in a world of limits. Our desires stretch beyond what this life can hold, and our understanding cannot explain why. Yet within that tension lies wisdom. When we stop pretending to control time, wealth, or meaning, we are finally free to receive life as it is—fragile, fleeting, and full of grace.

Qohelet does not promise satisfaction through simplicity; he calls for surrender through humility. The only cure for the unfulfilled life is to rest in the Giver rather than the gifts. When we accept that everything under the sun is vapor, we discover that gratitude alone has weight.

APPLICATION

1. Recognize that prosperity without gratitude is a curse

Qohelet's portrait of the rich man who "lacks nothing" yet cannot enjoy his blessings confronts one of life's harshest truths: abundance without gratitude leads to misery. God alone gives the power to enjoy, not merely to possess. Without that gift, even wealth becomes a burden. Modern Christians face the same temptation—to equate comfort with contentment. Yet comfort can numb the soul to dependence on God. The antidote is gratitude. Each moment of enjoyment—food, rest, laughter—is grace, not entitlement. When thanksgiving becomes our reflex, joy returns as gift rather than goal. A heart trained in gratitude transforms prosperity into praise and scarcity into peace. Without gratitude, possessions own us; with it, they become reminders of God's generosity.

2. Learn that life's length means little without satisfaction

Qohelet imagines a man with a hundred children and a thousand years to enjoy them—and still calls his life tragic if joy is missing. The message is clear: time and success cannot manufacture meaning. We may measure life in years, but God measures it in faithfulness. A long, joyless existence accomplishes nothing eternal. The stillborn child, in Qohelet's comparison, knows rest while the discontented never do. This stark contrast forces us to ask what makes life worthwhile. The answer is not longevity but fulfillment rooted in God. To live briefly yet gratefully is better than to live long and joyless. True significance comes not from duration but devotion. When contentment anchors our days, even short lives echo with eternal meaning.

3. Practice contentment in a world of constant craving

"All the toil of man is for his mouth, yet his appetite is not satisfied." Qohelet's proverb could headline any modern advertisement. Our world thrives on discontent; it sells the illusion that satisfaction waits just beyond the next purchase or achievement. But Ecclesiastes exposes that illusion: desire without discipline devours peace. Contentment begins when we learn to enjoy "the sight of the eyes"—the blessings already before us. Gratitude does not eliminate ambition; it redeems it. Instead of chasing the wind of what we lack, we rest in what God has provided. Practicing contentment is not resignation; it is resistance against the tyranny of more. The Christian who learns to say "enough" testifies that God is sufficient. Satisfaction cannot be stored or scheduled; it must be savored as gift in the present moment.

4. Rest in God's sovereignty when answers elude you

Qohelet ends with humility: "Who knows what is good for man…? Who can tell him what will be after him?" These questions silence human arrogance. We cannot control outcomes or predict tomorrow. The wise do not demand explanations; they trust the God who holds both time and eternity. Faith does not remove uncertainty—it redeems it. The one "stronger than we" is not fate but the Creator who names and orders all things. To rest in his sovereignty is to exchange anxiety for worship. When we accept that understanding is not required for obedience, peace replaces striving. Ecclesiastes 6 teaches that mystery is not our enemy but our teacher. Each unanswered question becomes an invitation to reverence, reminding us that joy is found not in knowing everything, but in knowing the One who does.

CONCLUSION

The Teacher's words pierce our illusions of control. Wealth cannot buy peace, success cannot secure joy, and knowledge cannot unlock mystery. Yet Qohelet does not end in cynicism—he points us to worship. The unfulfilled life becomes fulfilled only when it surrenders to the Giver. Gratitude turns futility into fellowship.

As the book turns to chapter 7, the Teacher shifts from frustration to reflection. There, he will explore the paradoxes of wisdom—how mourning teaches more than laughter, and rebuke refines more than praise. Ecclesiastes 6 exposes the limits of satisfaction; chapter 7 will reveal the path to understanding. Both remind us that life's greatest riches are found not under the sun, but in the fear of God.

REFLECTION

1. Why can wealth and success never guarantee joy?
2. What is the difference between possessing and enjoying life's blessings?
3. How does gratitude transform even small blessings into grace?
4. Why does discontentment rob both the rich and poor alike?
5. What limits of life are hardest for you to accept?
6. How can mystery deepen your trust in God's sovereignty?

DISCUSSION

1. What emotions arise when you read that a stillborn child is "better off" than the wealthy?
2. How does modern culture encourage the "wandering of the appetite"?
3. What habits help you practice contentment and gratitude daily?
4. Why is satisfaction ultimately more spiritual than circumstantial?
5. How can Christians model trust when they don't understand God's plan?
6. What does Ecclesiastes 6 teach about where joy truly comes from?

7

WHEN GOOD SENSE MEETS HARD LIFE

ECCLESIASTES 7

Objective: To learn to face life's hardships with humility, patience, and trust in God's wisdom.

INTRODUCTION

A pearl begins as irritation. A grain of sand lodges inside an oyster, and what could destroy it instead becomes something beautiful. The oyster covers the pain with layer after layer of nacre until the wound shines. Wisdom, Qohelet says, is born the same way—when irritation meets patience, and pain meets faith.

Chapter 7 marks a turning point in Ecclesiastes. The Teacher moves from exposing vanity to exploring wisdom—not as philosophy, but as survival. He teaches that sorrow can refine more than laughter, rebuke can heal more than praise, and patience can guard against pride. The heart that fears God learns how to walk through life's contradictions without losing balance.

Qohelet's wisdom feels countercultural because it is. Our world celebrates comfort, speed, and success; he celebrates humility, endurance, and reverence. He shows that good sense alone cannot guarantee good times, but it can steady us when life is hard. The wise do not avoid grief or mystery—they meet both with faith.

EXAMINATION

Wisdom and the value of adversity (7:1–4)

"A good name is better than precious ointment, and the day of death than the day of birth." The Teacher opens with a collection of paradoxical proverbs. A good reputation—*shem* in Hebrew—outlasts luxury. Just as fragrance lingers after perfume fades, integrity outlasts beauty or wealth. Qohelet's comparison links moral worth with permanence: a name endures when possessions vanish.

But the second half of the verse surprises: "The day of death is better than the day of birth." Qohelet does not glorify death but recognizes that mortality gives life its weight. Birth begins uncertainty; death completes the story and reveals its character. This sober realism runs through the chapter. Wisdom is not the ability to avoid sorrow but to interpret it rightly.

"It is better to go to the house of mourning than to go to the house of feasting." Funerals teach what parties conceal. The wise learn from loss; fools distract themselves with pleasure. The "living lay it to heart," meaning they internalize the lesson of mortality. "Sorrow is better than laughter," Qohelet continues, "for by sadness of face the heart is made glad." Pain, properly faced, produces depth. "The heart of the wise is in the house of mourning," he concludes, "but the heart of fools is in the house of mirth."

Ecclesiastes overturns shallow optimism. Hardship refines character; comfort dulls it. Wisdom begins not with success but with sobriety about life's brevity.

Rebuke, patience, and perspective (7:5–10)

"It is better for a man to hear the rebuke of the wise than to hear the song of fools." The contrast between correction and entertainment underscores a key theme: wisdom grows through humility. Fools prefer applause to accountability. "The laughter of fools is like the crackling of thorns under a pot"—brief, noisy, and useless. The fire flares but produces no heat. So too, shallow joy burns bright and dies quickly.

Qohelet warns that even the wise can be corrupted: "Surely oppression drives the wise into madness, and a bribe corrupts the heart." Power and greed distort judgment. The Teacher reminds us that integrity is fragile.

He continues with a proverb of endurance: "Better is the end of a thing than its beginning, and the patient in spirit than the proud in spirit." The end reveals purpose; patience allows perspective. Impatience mistakes process for failure, while pride resists waiting on God's timing. "Be not quick in your spirit to become angry, for anger lodges in the bosom of fools." Anger is impatience intensified—the refusal to accept limits or delays.

Finally, Qohelet cautions against nostalgia: "Say not, 'Why were the former days better than these?' For it is not from wisdom that you ask this." Every generation romanticizes its past, forgetting that folly and frustration have always existed. Wisdom accepts the present as God's appointed season, not as decline or disappointment.

Wisdom as protection and limitation (7:11–14)

"Wisdom is good with an inheritance, an advantage to those who see the sun." Like money, wisdom can preserve life, but unlike money, it cannot be stolen. "The protection of wisdom is like the protection of money, but the advantage of knowledge is that wisdom preserves the life of him who has it." Here, Qohelet affirms wisdom's practical value—it shields the prudent from danger, grants foresight, and sustains moral resilience.

Yet wisdom's usefulness is not limitless. "Consider the work of God: who can make straight what he has made crooked?" The Teacher echoes 1:15. Wisdom can interpret life but cannot alter its shape. The "crooked" may refer to adversity, loss, or mystery—the things beyond human correction. God's sovereignty sets boundaries wisdom cannot cross.

"In the day of prosperity be joyful, and in the day of adversity consider: God has made the one as well as the other." Joy and hardship both come from God's hand. Wisdom recognizes the divine rhythm and refuses to idolize either comfort or control. "So that man may not find out anything that will be after him." God's balance of good and bad events preserves humility. The wise live not by certainty but by trust.

Moderation in righteousness and wickedness (7:15–18)

"In my vain life I have seen everything: there is a righteous man who perishes in his righteousness, and a wicked man who prolongs his life in his evil-doing." Qohelet confronts a troubling reality: moral outcomes often defy expectation. The simplistic equation of righteousness with reward and wickedness with ruin collapses under experience.

"Be not overly righteous, and do not make yourself too wise. Why should you destroy yourself?" The warning is not against virtue but against presumption. "Overly righteous" describes self-righteousness—a legalistic attempt to manipulate God through moral performance. The "too wise" person trusts intellect over humility. Both forms of extremism destroy the soul.

Conversely, "Be not overly wicked, neither be a fool. Why should you die before your time?" The Teacher rejects license as much as legalism. The wise person "grabs hold of the one and does not let go of the other, for the one who fears God shall come out from both of them." The fear of God provides balance between self-righteous rigor and reckless sin. The wise avoid both despair and presumption, walking humbly between the ditches.

Wisdom's strength and humanity's weakness (7:19–22)

"Wisdom gives strength to the wise more than ten rulers who are in a city." Here, Qohelet affirms that true discernment surpasses political power. A single wise person can preserve a community better than a council of fools. Yet even the wise are not sinless: "Surely there is not a righteous man on earth who does good and never sins."

The Teacher warns against hypersensitivity to criticism: "Do not take to heart all the things that people say, lest you hear your servant cursing you. Your heart knows that many times you yourself have cursed others." Wisdom requires both moral realism and self-awareness. Human frailty is universal; the wise learn mercy from memory. If we expect perfection from others, we will drown in disappointment. Qohelet's humility anticipates the gospel truth that all have sinned. Awareness of imperfection should produce gentleness, not cynicism.

The limits of wisdom and the mystery of evil (7:23–29)

"All this I have tested by wisdom. I said, 'I will be wise,' but it was far from me." The Teacher's confession mirrors his conclusion in 1:13–18. Despite exhaustive searching, true wisdom eludes him. "That which has been is far off, and deep, very deep; who can find it out?" Qohelet's pursuit ends in awe—knowledge deepens mystery rather than dissolving it.

He turns to examine moral folly through a personal lens: "I find something more bitter than death: the woman whose heart is snares and nets, and whose hands are fetters. He who pleases God escapes her, but the sinner is taken by her." The "woman" symbolizes temptation or personified folly (see Prov. 7), not a specific individual. Qohelet warns that moral seduction—whether through desire, greed, or idolatry—ensnares the unguarded soul.

"See, this is what I found," he continues, "while adding one thing to another to find the scheme of things, which my soul has sought repeatedly, but I have not found." The Teacher's investigative metaphor ("adding one thing to another") conveys exhaustive analysis, yet his conclusion is frustration: "One man among a thousand I have found, but a woman among all these I have not found." This hyperbolic statement reflects exasperation, not misogyny. It laments the rarity of wisdom and integrity in humanity, not the worth of one gender. Qohelet's point is universal: the wise person—male or female—is exceedingly rare.

He concludes, "See, this alone I found, that God made man upright, but they have sought out many schemes." Humanity's problem is not divine design but human distortion. God created goodness; human ingenuity invented evil. Wisdom cannot undo corruption—it can only expose it. The more we study the world's moral complexity, the more we see our need for divine grace.

Humility as the heart of wisdom

Ecclesiastes 7 reshapes our understanding of wisdom. It is not control over life but surrender within it. The wise mourn sincerely, receive correction gratefully, wait patiently, and live reverently. They understand that adversity refines, prosperity tests, and righteousness without humility destroys.

Qohelet's hard-won insight is simple yet profound: wisdom's strength lies in its humility. To fear God is to embrace both joy and grief as gifts from the same hand. To pursue wisdom is to accept limits without losing wonder. In a world that prizes certainty, Ecclesiastes reminds believers that the truest knowledge begins with reverent unknowing—the moment when good sense meets hard life and still trusts God.

APPLICATION

1. Let adversity deepen your wisdom

Qohelet's paradoxes—mourning over feasting, rebuke over laughter—teach that pain can polish the heart. The "house of mourning" is not punishment; it is preparation. Adversity exposes illusions of control and invites us to see life as gift, not guarantee. God often speaks most clearly in quiet grief, when our distractions have been stripped away. Instead of resenting hardship, the wise ask what it reveals about God and themselves. True growth rarely comes from ease. The Teacher's insight aligns with later revelation: even Christ was made "perfect through suffering" (Heb. 2:10). When we face sorrow with faith, we learn humility, empathy, and endurance. The fool hides from pain; the wise person lets it become a teacher. Every valley walked with God becomes a classroom for grace.

2. Receive correction with humility and patience

"It is better to hear the rebuke of the wise than the song of fools." Qohelet's counsel reminds us that correction is a gift, not an insult. Pride resists it, but humility welcomes it as a safeguard for the soul. In an age allergic to criticism, wisdom grows through teachability. To accept reproof requires patience—the ability to hear hard truth without defending ourselves. God often refines us through voices we would rather ignore. The one who listens to rebuke learns discernment and compassion; the one who rejects it repeats mistakes. Wisdom begins where defensiveness ends. When we let correction wound our pride, it heals our perspective.

3. Live with balance, not extremes

Qohelet warns against both moral arrogance and reckless indulgence: "Be not overly righteous… be not overly wicked." Wisdom avoids both self-righteousness and self-destruction. Legalism destroys joy; license destroys holiness. The fear of God anchors Christians between these two cliffs. The wise neither excuse sin nor imagine perfection—they walk humbly, aware of both grace and weakness. In a polarized world that rewards extremes, Ecclesiastes calls for moderation rooted in reverence. Maturity means learning to live faithfully in tension, to hold conviction without condemnation, to pursue righteousness without pride. Balance is not compromise; it is composure under grace. When we fear God more than failure, we stop chasing perfection and start cultivating peace.

4. Accept mystery as part of faith

The Teacher confesses that even after exhaustive searching, "wisdom was far from me." His humility models mature faith. God's ways remain "deep, very deep"—beyond analysis. Believers are not called to decode every injustice or understand every trial. We are called to trust the One who governs both. The wise live comfortably with questions because they know who holds the answers. Mystery humbles the intellect but strengthens the heart. Faith that demands constant explanation soon collapses; faith that rests in God's sovereignty endures. When we reach the limits of reason, worship begins. Ecclesiastes invites us to trade anxiety for awe—to marvel at the God whose thoughts are higher than ours. In that reverent unknowing, peace quietly replaces pride.

CONCLUSION

Ecclesiastes 7 shows that wisdom is not escape from pain but endurance through it. The house of mourning teaches perspective, correction deepens humility, and mystery cultivates reverence. The wise accept that not all crooked things can be made straight—and trust the God who governs both joy and sorrow.

As the book moves into chapter 8, the Teacher will apply this wisdom to life under authority. He will ask how believers should live in a world where power seems unjust and timing unpredictable. But the principle remains the same: when good sense meets hard life, the fear of God keeps us steady beneath the sun.

REFLECTION

1. Why does Qohelet value mourning more than laughter?
2. How can sorrow strengthen faith instead of destroying it?
3. What makes humility essential for receiving correction?
4. How does the fear of God protect us from extremes?
5. What does Ecclesiastes teach about the limits of wisdom?
6. How can mystery draw us nearer to God rather than frustrate us?

DISCUSSION

1. When have you learned the most through adversity?
2. How does rebuke differ from criticism in the life of faith?
3. Why do people today struggle to live with balance and moderation?
4. What does healthy fear of God look like in daily decisions?
5. How can Christians embrace questions without losing confidence in Scripture?
6. What modern examples show the danger of pride disguised as wisdom?

8

WHEN WICKED MEN WIN

ECCLESIASTES 8

Objective: To learn to remain calm, joyful, and faithful when injustice seems to prevail.

INTRODUCTION

A Christian missionary once stood before a firing squad in China during the 1900 Boxer Rebellion. As the soldiers raised their rifles, he began to sing quietly, "Jesus loves me, this I know." The officer hesitated, ordered the rifles lowered, and the man was released. When asked why he sang, the missionary replied, "I wanted the last sound they heard to be peace."

That calm courage captures Qohelet's vision of wisdom in Ecclesiastes 8. The Teacher has seen injustice triumph, rulers abuse power, and the wicked receive honor they never earned. Yet instead of despair, he commends serenity, trust, and joy. Wisdom does not erase evil; it steadies the soul in its midst.

Chapter 8 teaches Christians how to live faithfully when wicked men win—how to respect authority without idolatry, to trust divine justice when human systems fail, and to rejoice as an act of rebellion against despair. The wise face life's moral puzzles with humility, hope, and holy calm.

EXAMINATION

The wisdom of composure (8:1)

"Who is like the wise? And who knows the interpretation of a thing?" Qohelet opens with praise for wisdom's quiet strength. The wise person is not defined by intellect alone but by discernment—the ability to "interpret" life's riddles without panic. Wisdom, he says, "makes a man's face shine, and the hardness of his face is changed." The image suggests that insight softens disposition. A wise person exudes calm in confusion, serenity in chaos.

In Hebrew thought, a radiant face often reflects divine favor (Num. 6:25). The Teacher implies that true wisdom grants the same peace: understanding that life's enigmas, though unresolved, are still under God's rule. Those who learn to trust rather than control wear a gentler countenance. Wisdom does not erase tension; it humanizes us within it.

Obeying power with prudence (8:2–6)

"I say: keep the king's command, because of God's oath to him." Qohelet turns from private reflection to public life. His counsel, like Proverbs and later Paul's in Romans 13, calls for respect toward authority—but his tone is pragmatic, not idealistic. Obedience to rulers is wise not because they are flawless, but because resistance often ends badly for the powerless.

"Be not hasty to go from his presence. Do not take your stand in an evil cause, for he does whatever pleases him." Ancient courts depended on favor; rash defiance could invite death. The Teacher observes political reality; he does not endorse tyranny. Human rulers wield temporary, imperfect power, yet wisdom teaches restraint—patience where impulse demands rebellion.

"For the word of the king is supreme, and who may say to him, 'What are you doing?'" The rhetorical question echoes humanity's posture before God himself. Earthly kings may act unjustly, but they remind us—by contrast—of heaven's true sovereignty. "Whoever keeps a command will know no evil thing, and the wise heart will know the proper time and the just way." Wisdom is not blind submission; it discerns when to act and when to wait.

"For there is a time and a way for everything, although man's trouble lies heavy on him." The phrase recalls 3:1–8: every matter has its appointed time. The wise recognize that even injustice will meet its season of reckoning. Trust in God's timing, not political perfection, becomes the mark of spiritual maturity.

The limits of human control (8:7–9)

"For he does not know what is to be, for who can tell him how it will be?" Qohelet returns to his favorite theme: the limits of human foresight. We cannot predict outcomes, much less manage them. "No man has power to retain the spirit, or power over the day of death." The Hebrew word *ruah* can mean both "breath" and "spirit," linking mortality to divine sovereignty. Humans cannot control breath, death, or destiny.

"There is no discharge in war, nor will wickedness deliver those who are given to it." Life is like a battle we cannot escape; every soldier must fight until death. Sin itself becomes a prison, not a refuge.

Qohelet reflects: "All this I observed while applying my heart to all that is done under the sun, when man had power over man to his hurt." Power often corrupts both the ruler and the ruled. The Teacher's realism cuts through idealism: injustice is not anomaly but pattern. Yet his observation carries a quiet call to endurance. Since we cannot control the future, wisdom teaches contentment and courage within it.

The enigma of injustice (8:10–13)

"Then I saw the wicked buried—they used to go in and out of the holy place and were praised in the city where they had done such things." The Teacher laments moral absurdity: the wicked receive honor in death, even from religious institutions. Corruption often masquerades as piety. Those who exploit others still occupy pews, still receive eulogies. "This also is vanity."

"Because the sentence against an evil deed is not executed speedily, the heart of the children of man is fully set to do evil." Delay in justice emboldens sin. When consequences seem absent, rebellion multiplies. Qohelet's frustration mirrors that of Habakkuk and the psalmists: why does God wait while wickedness prospers?

Yet he affirms what faith must cling to: "Though a sinner does evil a hundred times and prolongs his life, yet I know that it will be well with those who fear God, because they fear before him." The phrase "I know" signals conviction amid contradiction. Experience may not display justice, but faith declares it. "It will not be well with the wicked, neither will he prolong his days like a shadow, because he does not fear before God." Delay is not denial. Divine patience is mercy, not neglect. Justice deferred is still justice divine.

Qohelet's theology is not naive optimism; it is hard-won trust. The fear of God anchors the Christian when appearances deceive.

The riddle of reversed outcomes (8:14–15)

"There is a vanity that takes place on earth: that there are righteous people to whom it happens according to the deeds of the wicked, and wicked people to whom it happens according to the deeds of the righteous." Here the Teacher confronts life's moral inversion. The righteous suffer, the wicked thrive. The world does not function by formulas.

Yet instead of despair, Qohelet responds with his recurring refrain: "And I commend joy, for man has no good thing under the sun but to eat and drink and be joyful, for this will go with him in his toil through the days of his life that God has given him under the sun."

When life's scales refuse to balance, gratitude becomes rebellion against despair. Joy affirms that God's gifts still shine even when human systems fail. The Teacher's "commendation" of joy is not escapism; it is faith in disguise. To eat, drink, and rejoice "under the sun" is to trust that life, though fleeting, remains holy because it comes from the hand of God.

The mystery of God's work (8:16–17)

"When I applied my heart to know wisdom and to see the business that is done on earth—how neither day nor night do one's eyes see sleep—then I saw all the work of God, that man cannot find out the work that is done under the sun."

Qohelet closes the chapter where true wisdom begins: with confession. Despite relentless study, sleepless pursuit, and careful observation, he cannot comprehend God's providence. "However much man may toil in seeking, he will not find it out. Even though a wise man claims to know, he cannot find it out."

This humility completes the arc of the book's theology. The mystery of God is not failure of reason but invitation to faith. The wise recognize that understanding is partial, justice is postponed, and life remains vapor—but God's sovereignty endures.

Wisdom's posture under injustice

This chapter paints a portrait of faith under pressure. The Teacher does not explain injustice; he teaches how to live faithfully within it. The wise respect authority without worshiping it, endure evil without surrendering to cynicism, and rejoice in God's gifts without needing all the answers.

Qohelet's wisdom balances realism and reverence. Life is crooked, but God is not. Justice may sleep, but it will wake. When wicked men win and the righteous suffer, the wise choose awe over anger, patience over panic, and gratitude over bitterness. That is the posture of true wisdom under the sun.

Ecclesiastes 8 therefore calls Christians to calm obedience, patient endurance, and joyful trust. When wicked men win, the wise still fear God, enjoy his gifts, and wait for the day when hidden things are made clear.

APPLICATION

1. Practice wisdom with calm obedience

Qohelet's command to "keep the king's word" reminds believers that wisdom includes composure under authority. The Teacher doesn't endorse corruption—he advocates prudence. Rash rebellion often causes more harm than reform. God's people respect order not because rulers are righteous, but because God remains sovereign. In every era, the wise recognize that obedience and discernment can coexist. We live peaceably, yet truthfully, under imperfect systems while trusting that divine justice will prevail. Calm obedience does not mean silent complicity; it means steady faith when others panic. The radiant face of wisdom shines not through power, but patience. Christians honor God best when they obey conscientiously, speak respectfully, and live as reminders that ultimate authority belongs not to kings, presidents, or judges—but to the King of heaven.

2. Trust God's justice when the wicked prosper

Ecclesiastes confronts the disturbing sight of the wicked buried with honor and the righteous forgotten. The Teacher does not pretend the world is fair—he insists that faith survives when fairness fails. "Though a sinner does evil a hundred times," he says, "I know it will be well with those who fear God." Justice may seem delayed, but delay is not denial. God's patience reveals mercy; his judgment will reveal righteousness. The wise refuse to equate temporary success with divine approval. When wicked men win, they win only for a moment; eternity still belongs to the righteous. To trust God's justice is to live as though the final verdict has already been announced. The Christian who fears God can rest without resentment, knowing that grace will outlast every grave.

3. Choose joy as an act of faith

When Qohelet "commends joy," he's not ignoring injustice—he's overcoming it. Joy, in Ecclesiastes, is rebellion against despair. The Teacher calls believers to eat, drink, and rejoice because gratitude resists the darkness of cynicism. To delight in daily gifts—food, work, friendship—is to declare that evil cannot cancel goodness. Every meal shared in thanksgiving, every smile offered in hardship, testifies that God's world still contains beauty. Joy becomes a form of protest against meaninglessness. The fool chases pleasure to escape pain; the wise receive joy as grace amid it. Ecclesiastes 8 invites us to stop waiting for perfect conditions and start celebrating God's presence now. Joy is not denial—it's devotion.

4. Rest in mystery and walk by faith

Qohelet ends the chapter confessing that even wisdom cannot decipher God's ways. "Man cannot find out the work that is done under the sun." Yet ignorance does not equal abandonment. The inability to explain does not erase the ability to trust. Faith flourishes precisely where understanding fails. The wise acknowledge mystery not as obstacle but as evidence of divine greatness. God's purposes run deeper than our logic, and his justice broader than our senses. To rest in mystery is to live with humility and hope—to stop demanding answers and start delighting in the Answerer. When we cannot trace God's hand, we trust his heart. Ecclesiastes teaches that serenity is not found in knowing everything, but in surrendering to the One who does.

CONCLUSION

Ecclesiastes 8 refuses to pretend that life is fair—but it also refuses to surrender faith. The wicked may prosper, but their victory is temporary. The wise rest in God's sovereignty, finding peace not in control but in trust. When the world praises evil and mocks righteousness, believers answer with quiet confidence and thankful joy.

In chapter 9, Qohelet will carry this wisdom into life's most sobering truth—death. There he will ask how the certainty of dying can teach us to live. For now, he leaves us with this lesson: when wicked men win, faith does not falter; it shines.

REFLECTION

1. Why is wisdom often seen in quietness rather than control?
2. What does it mean to "keep the king's word" with discernment?
3. How can faith endure when the wicked seem to prosper?
4. Why is joy a powerful act of faith amid injustice?
5. What limits of life remind you most of God's sovereignty?
6. How can mystery strengthen faith instead of weakening it?

DISCUSSION

1. What does wisdom look like in an unjust or corrupt system today?
2. How can Christians show respect for authority without endorsing wrongdoing?
3. Why does Ecclesiastes link joy and fear of God so closely?
4. How do delayed consequences encourage or discourage moral behavior?
5. What daily habits help you resist bitterness when life seems unfair?
6. How can humility help you live peacefully with unanswered questions?

9

EAT, DRINK, & REMEMBER
ECCLESIASTES 9

Objective: To learn to embrace joy, humility, and diligence as faithful responses to life's brevity.

INTRODUCTION

A few years ago, a hospice nurse published reflections from her patients on what they most regretted as they approached death. No one wished they had worked longer hours or earned more money. Nearly all said they wished they had laughed more, lingered longer with people they loved, and learned to enjoy ordinary days while they still could.

That perspective captures the heartbeat of Ecclesiastes 9. After confronting the injustice of chapter 8, Qohelet turns his gaze from what frustrates faith to what sustains it. He does not pretend that life is fair or that death can be delayed; instead, he insists that joy is still possible—indeed, commanded. "Go, eat your bread with joy and drink your wine with a merry heart, for God has already approved what you do."

Here, the Teacher gathers the wisdom of the entire book into a single truth: mortality gives meaning, not futility, to our days. Because life is short, gratitude must be urgent. Because death is certain, joy must be deliberate. Bread, wine, love, and labor become sacred gifts when received from God's hand.

Ecclesiastes 9 is not a hymn to pleasure but to perspective. The Teacher calls us to live each day as a divine invitation—to celebrate what we cannot keep, to cherish what we still have, and to remember the God who gives purpose even to life's vapor.

EXAMINATION

The sovereignty of God and the uncertainty of life (9:1-3)

Qohelet begins this chapter by gathering all his reflections into a single premise: "But all this I laid to heart, examining it all, how the righteous and the wise and their deeds are in the hand of God." Here, sovereignty replaces certainty. The righteous cannot predict outcomes; they can only rest in God's providence. "Whether it is love or hate, man does not know; both are before him." Love and hate here represent fortune and adversity, not divine emotion. Life's outcomes remain hidden even from the faithful.

"All things come alike to all." Death levels all distinctions—righteous and wicked, clean and unclean, devout and irreligious. Qohelet names this reality "an evil under the sun." In a world governed by mortality, outcomes do not always match deeds. Even piety offers no exemption. "The hearts of the children of man are full of evil, and madness is in their hearts while they live, and after that they go to the dead." Humanity's shared corruption makes death both universal and deserved, but its indiscriminate timing feels unjust.

Qohelet's lament is not disbelief but honesty. He refuses to deny the tension between divine sovereignty and human experience. The wise recognize that everything lies "in the hand of God"—even what they cannot explain.

Hope amid mortality (9:4-6)

"But he who is joined with all the living has hope, for a living dog is better than a dead lion." In the ancient Near East, dogs symbolized shame and uncleanness; lions, majesty and strength. Qohelet overturns the comparison—life, however humble, is better than grandeur in the grave. The living still possess possibility.

"For the living know that they will die, but the dead know nothing." Death ends consciousness and participation in earthly affairs. Qohelet is not denying eternal life but describing reality "under the sun"—the visible realm of time and mortality. "They have no more reward, for the memory of them is forgotten." Death erases status and cuts off all human connection: "Their love and their hate and their envy have already perished."

The Teacher's realism deflates pride but exalts gratitude. To be alive is to have opportunity—to act, repent, enjoy, and believe. Awareness of mortality, far from despairing, awakens urgency. The wise learn to cherish time not because it lasts, but because it doesn't.

Joy as divine gift (9:7–10)

"Go, eat your bread with joy, and drink your wine with a merry heart, for God has already approved what you do." This imperative marks one of the book's brightest refrains. After confronting death, Qohelet commends life. The command "Go" suggests deliberate, active joy. Bread and wine symbolize daily sustenance and celebration. God's prior approval does not imply moral perfection but divine invitation: joy is permitted, even commanded, for the righteous who fear him.

"Let your garments always be white; let not oil be lacking on your head." White garments represented festivity and purity; oil symbolized vitality and blessing. The Teacher's imagery portrays life as a feast, not a funeral. Joy does not deny death—it shines brighter against it.

"Enjoy life with the wife whom you love, all the days of your vain life that he has given you under the sun." Marriage becomes a metaphor for companionship and grace amid impermanence. Qohelet is not cynical in calling life "vain"; he means vapor—fleeting yet beautiful. "Whatever your hand finds to do, do it with your might, for there is no work or thought or knowledge or wisdom in Sheol, to which you are going." Death limits opportunity, so diligence is the only wise response.

Qohelet's joy is realistic, not naïve. Life is vapor, but vapor can shimmer in sunlight. The command to eat, drink, and love sanctifies the present moment as sacred space for gratitude.

The race is not to the swift (9:11–12)

"Again I saw that under the sun the race is not to the swift, nor the battle to the strong, nor bread to the wise, nor riches to the intelligent, nor favor to those with knowledge, but time and chance happen to them all." This verse shatters human illusions of control. Talent and strategy may shape outcomes, but providence decides them.

The Hebrew term for "chance" (*pega'*) suggests an encounter—unplanned, unpredictable, divine interruption. "Man does not know his time," Qohelet continues. "Like fish taken in an evil net, and like birds caught in a snare, so the children of man are snared in an evil time when it suddenly falls upon them." The imagery emphasizes surprise and fragility.

Qohelet's tone is not despairing but cautionary. Life resists calculation. Wisdom can prepare but not predict. The swift runner may stumble; the slow one may finish first. God's providence, not probability, rules outcomes. The lesson is humility—do your work with excellence, but never mistake effort for sovereignty.

The quiet strength of wisdom (9:13–16)

"I have also seen this example of wisdom under the sun, and it seemed great to me." Qohelet tells a brief parable: "There was a little city with few men in it, and a great king came against it and besieged it, building great siegeworks against it. But there was found in it a poor, wise man, and he by his wisdom delivered the city. Yet no one remembered that poor man."

This story captures the paradox of wisdom: powerful in effect but fragile in reputation. The Teacher concludes, "Wisdom is better than might, though the poor man's wisdom is despised, and his words are not heard." Wisdom's strength lies not in fame but in faithfulness. It accomplishes quietly what strength cannot, even if the world forgets the one who offers it.

The parable prefigures Christlike humility: salvation through weakness, deliverance through disregard. Ecclesiastes thus honors not the celebrated hero but the faithful servant who does good even when unseen.

The fragility of influence (9:17–18)

"The words of the wise heard in quiet are better than the shouting of a ruler among fools." The Teacher ends with an antithesis between volume and value. True wisdom whispers; folly shouts. The wise speak carefully, their authority arising from truth, not noise.

"Wisdom is better than weapons of war, but one sinner destroys much good." Wisdom builds, while folly ruins. The final warning underscores the fragility of virtue: one act of evil can unravel years of good. Ecclesiastes' realism remains consistent—wisdom is precious but vulnerable. Its influence, though easily forgotten, remains God's chosen means of preserving life.

Faith, joy, and humility before death

Ecclesiastes 9 unites the book's great themes into a single melody of faith. Death is certain, life uncertain, yet both rest in God's hand. The wise do not seek control—they seek contentment. Joy becomes worship, work becomes devotion, and wisdom becomes quiet resistance to despair.

Qohelet's message is not resignation but release. Since we cannot command outcomes, we receive each day as gift. The call to "eat, drink, and be joyful" is not the cynic's creed—it is the believer's courage. To live well under the sun is to remember the God who rules above it, even when life feels as fragile as vapor.

APPLICATION

1. Live fully, knowing life is fragile

Qohelet's realism about death is not meant to crush joy but to awaken it. "The living know that they will die," he writes, and that knowledge becomes the foundation of gratitude. Every sunrise, every shared meal, every quiet evening with loved ones is a miracle disguised as routine. Death's certainty should not paralyze us; it should prioritize what matters. When we remember that time is short, we learn to invest it in things eternal—faith, love, mercy, and truth. The wise do not deny mortality; they steward life because of it. Each day under the sun is a temporary gift wrapped in divine purpose. To live fully is to stop waiting for ideal conditions and start rejoicing that God still gives breath, purpose, and grace today.

2. Receive joy as an act of obedience

When Qohelet says, "Go, eat your bread with joy," he's not advocating indulgence—he's commanding gratitude. The Teacher insists that joy is not optional for those who fear God. To delight in daily blessings is to honor the Giver. Joyless faith misrepresents a generous God. To wear white garments and anoint one's head with oil symbolizes celebration, not vanity. God "has already approved what you do," meaning he delights in his people's contentment when rooted in reverence. Joy becomes obedience when it flows from trust rather than denial. The Christian who smiles amid sorrow proclaims that goodness still reigns. Ecclesiastes teaches that holiness and happiness are not rivals but relatives—both born from the same faith that sees every gift as grace.

3. Work diligently while you can

"Whatever your hand finds to do, do it with your might." Qohelet's counsel turns mortality into motivation. Death limits opportunity, but it also dignifies effort. Because tomorrow is uncertain, the wise work faithfully today. Laziness wastes both time and trust. Whether the task is grand or humble, each moment of labor can become worship when done for God's glory. Work is not punishment for mortality; it is purpose within it. Qohelet reminds us that diligence is a form of gratitude—thankfulness expressed through excellence. The Christian's calling is not to control results but to give wholehearted effort while grace allows breath. Someday our hands will rest, but until then, we work with joy, knowing our labor "in the Lord is not in vain" (1 Cor. 15:58).

4. Walk humbly, for outcomes belong to God

"The race is not to the swift, nor the battle to the strong." Life refuses to follow human logic. Skill matters, but sovereignty decides. Ecclesiastes warns against trusting our abilities as guarantees. Wisdom teaches diligence, but humility remembers dependence. Success is gift, not entitlement; failure is lesson, not ruin. The believer walks humbly, accepting that God's providence governs all. Our task is to run faithfully, even when we cannot control the finish line. Pride demands predictability; faith thrives on trust. Qohelet invites us to rest in mystery, to work hard but worship harder. When we release outcomes to God, peace replaces pressure. We can eat, drink, and rejoice not because we hold tomorrow, but because the One who does is good.

CONCLUSION

Qohelet's wisdom in chapter 9 brings us to the heart of the book: life is fleeting, but grace is not. The certainty of death makes gratitude urgent, and joy becomes our act of trust. We cannot control time, chance, or outcome—but we can worship the God who governs them all.

As the book turns to chapter 10, the Teacher will explore how folly threatens that wisdom. Even a little foolishness can ruin a lifetime of good. Ecclesiastes 9 teaches us to live gratefully; chapter 10 will warn us to live carefully. Both truths belong together—joy with discernment, gratitude with guardrails—under the steady hand of God.

REFLECTION

1. What does it mean to say life is "in the hand of God"?
2. How does remembering death change the way we live today?
3. Why is joy an act of faith rather than emotion?
4. How can diligence become an expression of gratitude?
5. Why do outcomes belong to God and not to us?
6. What does true humility look like in everyday life?

DISCUSSION

1. How does Ecclesiastes 9 challenge modern views of success and control?
2. Why do you think God commands joy instead of simply permitting it?
3. What keeps people from enjoying the blessings they already have?
4. In what ways does work become worship for the believer?
5. How can Christians practice humility when life feels unpredictable?
6. What does Ecclesiastes teach about finding purpose amid mortality?

10

WISDOM IN THE STREETS
ECCLESIASTES 10

Objective: To guard against everyday folly by practicing calmness, preparation, and disciplined speech.

INTRODUCTION

In 2003, NASA lost a $125 million Mars Climate Orbiter before it ever reached its destination. The cause wasn't sabotage or system failure—it was a math mistake. One engineering team calculated using metric units while another used English measurements. The difference was just a few inches of thrust, but it sent the spacecraft fatally off course. Years of planning, data, and brilliance were undone by one overlooked detail. A tiny misalignment led to total disaster.

Qohelet would have nodded knowingly. Ecclesiastes 10 opens with the image of "dead flies in the perfumer's ointment," a picture of how something small and seemingly insignificant can spoil something precious. Wisdom builds slowly but can be ruined in a moment. A single careless word, an impulsive decision, or an unguarded attitude can destroy what took years to earn.

The lost orbiter reminds us that folly rarely begins with rebellion—it begins with neglect. The difference between a wise life and a foolish one often lies in inches, not miles. The wise person learns to pay attention to the small things: tone, timing, attitude, humility. Ecclesiastes 10 teaches that the fragrance of our character depends not on brilliance but on consistency. Wisdom doesn't require perfection, but it does require precision—a heart and mind calibrated daily to the fear of God.

EXAMINATION

The stench of folly (10:1)

"Dead flies make the perfumer's ointment give off a stench; so a little folly outweighs wisdom and honor." The Teacher opens with a vivid proverb. In the ancient world, perfumed oil was expensive and carefully crafted, symbolizing reputation or virtue. Yet even a few dead flies could spoil the fragrance. Qohelet's point is sobering: moral foolishness, though small, has disproportionate impact.

Wisdom builds slowly; folly destroys quickly. A single rash word, impulsive act, or selfish motive can corrupt years of integrity. Ecclesiastes reminds Christians that character is fragile and must be guarded with humility. The imagery also reflects moral decay: folly's rot is subtle but pervasive. As perfume once attracted, now it repels. The wise must therefore remain alert, for pride, impatience, or carelessness can turn virtue into vanity in a moment.

The direction of the heart (10:2-3)

"A wise man's heart inclines him to the right, but a fool's heart to the left." In Hebrew idiom, the "right" represented strength, protection, and skill; the "left" represented weakness or misfortune. Qohelet uses spatial imagery to show that wisdom and folly move in opposite directions. The "heart" denotes the seat of thought and will, not emotion. The wise think before acting; the fool reacts without reflection.

"Even when the fool walks on the road, he lacks sense, and he says to everyone that he is a fool." The Teacher mocks folly's visibility. A fool cannot hide himself; arrogance betrays him. His words and manner expose inner disorder. True wisdom is not merely intellect but orientation—a heart that leans toward righteousness rather than self. The wise walk with awareness; the fool stumbles publicly, convinced of his own insight.

Dealing with power and anger (10:4-7)

"If the anger of the ruler rises against you, do not leave your place, for calmness will lay great offenses to rest." Here, Qohelet counsels composure when under authority. Anger from a superior can provoke fear or retaliation, but the wise remain steady. "Calmness," or *marpē*, literally means "healing." A tranquil response can soothe tension more effectively than protest (see Prov. 15:1).

"There is an evil that I have seen under the sun, as it were an error proceeding from the ruler: folly is set in many high places, and the rich sit in a low place. I have seen slaves on horses, and princes walking on the ground like slaves." The Teacher laments political absurdity—positions of power filled by fools, while competence goes unrewarded. Yet his tone remains observational, not cynical. Life under the sun often reverses expectations, but wisdom calls for patience rather than outrage. Foolishness may occupy thrones, but it never dethrones God.

The dangers of carelessness (10:8-11)

"He who digs a pit will fall into it, and a serpent will bite him who breaks through a wall." This cluster of proverbs warns that carelessness—even in ordinary labor—invites harm. The imagery depicts workers acting without caution: demolishing walls without checking for snakes, splitting logs without foresight. Folly is not just moral failure; it is practical negligence.

"If the iron is blunt, and one does not sharpen the edge, he must use more strength, but wisdom helps one to succeed." Preparation and foresight make work fruitful. The fool exhausts himself through impatience; the wise conserve effort by reflection. Efficiency, in Qohelet's view, is a form of wisdom.

"If the serpent bites before it is charmed, there is no advantage to the charmer." Timing matters. Wisdom requires not only knowledge but discernment—the ability to act at the proper moment. Words or actions spoken out of season lose their power, like a charmer bitten by the very snake he sought to control.

The speech of fools (10:12-15)

"The words of a wise man's mouth win him favor, but the lips of a fool consume him." Qohelet now moves from behavior to speech, showing that folly often begins with the tongue. The wise use words to build trust; the foolish use them to self-destruct.

"The beginning of the words of his mouth is foolishness, and the end of his talk is evil madness." Folly escalates—what starts as ignorance ends in arrogance. "A fool multiplies words, though no man knows what is to be, and who can tell him what will be after him?" The fool's verbosity reflects delusion: he speaks with certainty about things only God can know.

"The toil of a fool wearies him, for he does not know the way to the city." This proverb paints the fool as hopelessly inept—so lost that he cannot find the main road. Wisdom simplifies; folly complicates. Those who talk endlessly often achieve little. The wise, by contrast, speak with brevity and act with direction.

Folly in leadership (10:16–17)

"Woe to you, O land, when your king is a child, and your princes feast in the morning! Happy are you, O land, when your king is the son of the free, and your princes feast at the proper time—for strength, and not for drunkenness!" Qohelet contrasts immature and mature leadership. The "child" king symbolizes inexperience, impulsiveness, and indulgence. His officials "feast in the morning," wasting the day's strength on pleasure rather than duty.

In contrast, the "son of the free"—a phrase implying noble character rather than lineage—governs with discipline. His leaders eat "for strength," not self-gratification. Wise governance prioritizes service; foolish governance prioritizes self. Ecclesiastes echoes the wisdom tradition that moral restraint sustains both leaders and nations.

The consequences of laziness and negligence (10:18–19)

"Through sloth the roof sinks in, and through indolence the house leaks." Laziness, whether in a home or a kingdom, leads to slow collapse. The proverb applies politically and personally. Neglect corrodes stability. What is left unattended eventually decays.

"Bread is made for laughter, and wine gladdens life, and money answers everything." This verse sounds cynical, but Qohelet likely describes pragmatic reality, not moral approval. Food, drink, and money sustain society's functions. Yet in context, the line critiques leaders who mistake luxury for leadership—those who believe material satisfaction can solve every problem. Wisdom enjoys blessings with moderation; folly trusts them for meaning.

Guarding the tongue (10:20)

"Even in your thoughts, do not curse the king, nor in your bedroom curse the rich, for a bird of the air will carry your voice, or some winged creature tell the matter." The Teacher closes with irony: private contempt often becomes public scandal. The proverb's humor—"a little bird told me"—carries serious warning. Words, once spoken, escape control.

Qohelet's wisdom transcends politics. He urges discretion, not deceit. Whether about rulers, employers, or friends, reckless speech returns to harm its speaker. The wise cultivate internal restraint: even thoughts require discipline. The fool vents every opinion; the wise weigh every word.

Wisdom that preserves and folly that destroys

Ecclesiastes 10 gathers the Teacher's sharpest contrasts between wisdom and folly. Folly spoils honor, exposes pride, provokes rulers, multiplies words, and corrupts leadership. Wisdom, by contrast, preserves life through patience, discipline, and discretion.

The chapter's realism reminds Christians that foolishness is not confined to the uneducated or irreligious—it lurks in every heart. Wisdom demands constant vigilance. Whether we lead or follow, speak or stay silent, work or rest, each decision reveals our direction: toward life or toward decay.

Qohelet's closing image—the bird carrying our careless words—summarizes his entire philosophy of wisdom: small things matter. A dead fly, a dull blade, a rash sentence—all seem minor until they ruin everything. The wise therefore live attentively, aware that faithfulness in the little things keeps the fragrance of their lives pleasing before God.

APPLICATION

1. Guard your character in the small things

Qohelet's proverb about "dead flies" reminds us that character rarely collapses suddenly—it erodes slowly. A small compromise can poison a lifetime of integrity. A careless word, a hidden indulgence, or a moment of pride may seem harmless, yet over time it produces the stench of folly.

The wise learn that holiness depends on attention to details no one else sees. Integrity is built in obscurity long before it is tested in public. God values faithfulness in the small because it reveals the state of the heart. The Christian who guards conscience in private preserves credibility in public. Wisdom whispers: do not underestimate the power of little things—for good or for evil. The fragrance of Christ is maintained by daily obedience, not occasional brilliance.

2. Stay calm when authority tests your spirit

When the ruler's anger rises, Qohelet says, "Do not leave your place." Wisdom's strength lies in composure. Anger—whether from a superior, a critic, or a peer—invites reaction, but the wise respond with restraint. Calmness defuses tension more effectively than outrage. The world equates leadership with dominance, but Scripture calls it patience under pressure. By refusing to react impulsively, the believer reflects confidence in God's control over circumstances. In an age of outrage, gentleness is revolutionary. To remain steady when provoked is not weakness but faith. The fool vents, the wise wait. When insulted or misunderstood, wisdom remembers: "A gentle answer turns away wrath." The calm heart becomes the healing presence in a chaotic world.

3. Sharpen your work through preparation and patience

"If the iron is blunt," Qohelet says, "more strength is needed, but wisdom helps one to succeed." The fool swings harder; the wise sharpen first. Preparation multiplies impact and honors God. In every vocation—whether teaching, parenting, preaching, or leading—the difference between weariness and fruitfulness is foresight. Planning, reflection, and prayer are not delays; they are investments. The fool sees waiting as wasted time; the wise see it as sharpening time. Likewise, wisdom discerns proper timing. Acting too soon can wound as surely as acting too late. Ecclesiastes invites us to measure effort by readiness, not restlessness. Our calling is not to rush but to refine. Diligence without direction only exhausts. The wise pause, pray, and then proceed, trusting that patient preparation is part of obedience.

4. Speak less, listen more, and honor others

"The words of the wise bring favor, but the lips of the fool consume him." Speech reveals character faster than action. The fool multiplies words; the wise measure them. Gossip, criticism, and complaint spread quickly, like birds carrying secrets into the open. Ecclesiastes warns us that every careless word eventually returns home. The wise discipline the tongue not by silence alone but by reverence—speaking only what builds up, not what tears down. To honor others with our words is to honor God with our hearts. Before speaking, wisdom asks, "Is this true? Is it kind? Is it necessary?" The fool speaks to be heard; the wise speak to help. Words are seeds—they either nourish or poison. The believer who learns restraint plants peace wherever they go.

CONCLUSION

Ecclesiastes 10 shows that foolishness isn't limited to loud sin—it is quiet neglect. A single unguarded word, a moment of pride, or a small compromise can spoil what years of faithfulness built. The wise live attentively, choosing restraint over reaction, diligence over distraction, and humility over haste.

As the Teacher turns to chapter 11, he will shift from the danger of folly to the discipline of faith—how to act boldly yet trust God with the outcome. Life remains uncertain, but wisdom equips us to live well in the midst of it. Until then, Ecclesiastes 10 reminds us: holiness often hides in the smallest decisions.

REFLECTION

1. Why does Qohelet compare folly to "dead flies"?
2. How does patience display strength rather than weakness?
3. What daily habits help you prepare your heart and work with wisdom?
4. Why do small words or actions carry such great influence?
5. How does your speech reveal the state of your heart?
6. What can you do this week to "sharpen the axe" in your life and work?

DISCUSSION

1. What modern examples show how small acts of folly ruin reputation?
2. How can calmness defuse anger or conflict in leadership situations?
3. Why is preparation a form of wisdom rather than procrastination?
4. What makes it difficult to guard our words in today's culture?
5. How can churches cultivate a community of careful, gracious speech?
6. How does this chapter point toward the need for God's grace in daily life?

11

CAST YOUR BREAD

ECCLESIASTES 11

Objective: To live courageously and joyfully, trusting God amid life's uncertainties and opportunities.

INTRODUCTION

In 1961, President John F. Kennedy announced that America would send a man to the moon and return him safely to earth—within the decade. At the time, NASA had barely launched a rocket beyond the atmosphere. The statement sounded impossible. But that single act of courage—choosing to begin before certainty—changed the course of history. Every breakthrough, Kennedy said, "starts with the decision to try."

Qohelet would have agreed. Ecclesiastes 11 opens with the call, "Cast your bread upon the waters." In other words, act. Give. Risk. Trust. Waiting for ideal conditions guarantees failure. The Teacher insists that life's unpredictability is not a reason for hesitation but an invitation to faith. The wise understand that God alone controls the outcome, but that truth doesn't excuse inaction—it empowers obedience.

This chapter shifts from reflection to movement. After observing life's frustrations and uncertainties, Qohelet now urges courage: sow seed in the morning, work in the evening, and rejoice in every day that God gives. Life under the sun is fragile, but faith was never meant to live in safety. The wise live boldly not because they know the future, but because they know the One who holds it. Ecclesiastes 11 is a hymn to active trust—a call to step forward even when the ground beneath us feels unsure.

EXAMINATION

Faithful risk and generous action (11:1–2)

"Cast your bread upon the waters, for you will find it after many days." The opening proverb invites bold, generous living in a world full of uncertainty. The image of casting bread—grain or seed—on the water evokes risk. In ancient trade, merchants would send goods overseas not knowing if they would return; farmers would sow seed in floodplains hoping the water would recede and growth would follow. Either way, the command calls for trust and initiative, not paralysis.

Qohelet's wisdom is not reckless but faithful. "Give a portion to seven, or even to eight, for you know not what disaster may happen on earth." The Teacher counsels generosity and diversification. Whether in charity, work, or investment, share widely because the future is unpredictable. Greed hoards; faith releases. Wisdom knows that life's unpredictability is not an excuse for fear but an invitation to courage. Since outcomes belong to God, the wise act in faith rather than freeze in doubt.

Accepting uncertainty under providence (11:3–6)

"If the clouds are full of rain, they empty themselves on the earth, and if a tree falls to the south or to the north, in the place where the tree falls, there it will lie." This proverb affirms both the certainty of natural order and the mystery of human limitation. Rain falls; trees topple—events occur beyond human control.

"He who observes the wind will not sow, and he who regards the clouds will not reap." Over-analysis leads to paralysis. Those who wait for perfect conditions never act. Wisdom requires courage to move forward even when outcomes are unclear. "As you do not know the way the spirit comes to the bones in the womb of a woman with child, so you do not know the work of God who makes everything." Human ignorance is not defect but design. Just as we cannot explain the mystery of life's beginning, we cannot predict providence's pattern.

"In the morning sow your seed, and at evening withhold not your hand, for you do not know which will prosper—this or that—or whether both alike will be good." The Teacher commends diligence and persistence. Because we "do not know," we must do. Uncertainty, properly understood, motivates action, not hesitation. The wise person lives with both humility and energy—trusting that God's unseen hand works through every effort offered in faith.

The goodness of life and the brevity of light (11:7–8)

"Light is sweet, and it is pleasant for the eyes to see the sun." After confronting risk and uncertainty, Qohelet returns to joy. Life, even in its imperfection, remains a gift to be savored. The word "sweet" suggests sensory delight, not naïve optimism. Every sunrise is an act of grace. The wise do not despise earthly pleasures; they receive them with reverence.

"So if a person lives many years, let him rejoice in them all, but let him remember that the days of darkness will be many. All that comes is vanity." Joy and sobriety coexist. The Teacher refuses both cynicism and denial. The days of darkness—suffering, aging, and death—are inevitable, yet they do not erase the sweetness of the light. Life's brevity should intensify, not diminish, gratitude. The one who fears God learns to celebrate both sunshine and shadow, knowing both come from his hand.

Rejoicing in youth and remembering accountability (11:9–10)

"Rejoice, O young man, in your youth, and let your heart cheer you in the days of your youth. Walk in the ways of your heart and the sight of your eyes." This is not permission for self-indulgence but invitation to joyful stewardship. God delights when his people embrace life fully, enjoying the strength, curiosity, and opportunity of youth. The Teacher's earlier cautions about vanity do not cancel joy—they frame it with wisdom.

"But know that for all these things God will bring you into judgment." Joy without reverence becomes recklessness. The fear of God transforms pleasure into praise. To live fully under the sun is to remember accountability under heaven. Every experience is a chance to honor the Creator through gratitude, creativity, and moral integrity.

"Remove vexation from your heart and put away pain from your body, for youth and the dawn of life are vanity." The Teacher urges freedom from bitterness and anxiety. "Vexation" here means resentment or cynicism; "pain" can mean moral evil or physical indulgence. Both corrupt joy. Youth is fleeting, like morning fog; to waste it in anger or excess is folly. The wise, whether young or old, enjoy life without idolizing it.

Qohelet's theology of joy is mature: pleasure and accountability, freedom and restraint, delight and reverence belong together. God's gifts are meant to be enjoyed responsibly because they are temporary, and that temporariness makes them sacred.

Bold faith in uncertain times

Ecclesiastes 11 gathers the Teacher's wisdom on how to live faithfully in a world of risk and unpredictability. Life cannot be controlled, only trusted. The wise act generously, labor diligently, rejoice freely, and remember soberly. They sow seed even when clouds gather, because they know the harvest depends on God.

The Teacher's message blends courage and humility: take chances, but trust providence; enjoy blessings, but remember accountability. Life under the sun is brief and uncertain, but it is also beautiful and worth living well. True faith does not eliminate risk—it sanctifies it. The one who fears God learns to act boldly, give freely, and rejoice deeply, knowing that the same God who governs the wind also blesses the work of faithful hands.

APPLICATION

1. Take faith-filled risks for God's glory

Qohelet's call to "cast your bread upon the waters" is a summons to courageous faith. Wisdom does not wait for perfect conditions; it obeys despite uncertainty. Too many Christian mistake caution for spirituality, forgetting that faith itself is risk—a trust placed beyond what we can see. Whether it's sharing the gospel, serving generously, or pursuing new work, the wise act boldly, trusting that God multiplies what we release. Fear keeps our seed in the barn; faith casts it into God's care. We will not know the harvest unless we scatter what we've been given. Life under the sun will always involve risk, but the greater danger is regret. When the winds seem unpredictable, the faithful sow anyway—because obedience is never wasted.

2. Work diligently, even when outcomes are uncertain

"He who observes the wind will not sow." Waiting for perfect timing paralyzes progress. Qohelet teaches that uncertainty is not an obstacle but a constant companion to faith. Wisdom plans, but it does not postpone. The wise farmer sows in the morning and again at evening, trusting God to decide what will prosper. Every day becomes an opportunity for faithfulness rather than fear. The Christian life is a rhythm of labor and trust—doing all we can and resting in all God will do. We do not control weather, results, or recognition, but we can control obedience. Diligence honors God precisely because it admits dependence. Our calling is not to guarantee success but to glorify God through steadfast effort, even when outcomes remain unseen.

3. Enjoy life's sweetness with gratitude and reverence

"Light is sweet," says Qohelet, "and it is pleasant for the eyes to see the sun." Even in a fallen world, life remains a miracle worth enjoying. Wisdom does not demand perfection before it rejoices. Every sunrise, every shared meal, every laugh with a friend is a divine reminder that existence itself is grace. Gratitude transforms ordinary pleasures into worship. Yet the Teacher balances joy with reverence: the days of darkness will come, and God will bring every deed into judgment. The key to wise enjoyment is not indulgence but awareness—delight tethered to devotion. To enjoy life's sweetness without losing sight of its brevity is true maturity. Joy without reverence is reckless; reverence without joy is lifeless. Wisdom learns to live between the two, giving thanks for each fleeting moment under the sun.

4. Rejoice in youth, remembering accountability before God

Qohelet calls the young to rejoice—but not to rebel. "Walk in the ways of your heart," he says, "but know that for all these things God will bring you into judgment." Joy and responsibility are not enemies; they are partners. Youth is a season of energy, curiosity, and opportunity—meant to be celebrated, not squandered. God delights in his children's gladness when it is anchored in gratitude. To "remove vexation" means to let go of resentment and cynicism before they harden the heart. Wise believers enjoy freedom without forgetting the Giver. True joy flows from remembering that God's judgment is not just punishment—it is the assurance that life has meaning and moral weight. When we live joyfully yet humbly before him, even our laughter becomes an offering of faith.

CONCLUSION

Ecclesiastes 11 calls Christians to a daring kind of wisdom. Life will never be predictable, but faith acts anyway. The Teacher's vision is not reckless but reverent: sow your seed, share your blessings, and savor the sunlight while remembering the God who governs it all.

As the book moves into chapter 12, Qohelet will bring this message to its climax—urging us to "remember your Creator in the days of your youth." The call to bold living now becomes a call to enduring faith. Life under the sun is fleeting, but when lived for the glory of God, it shines with eternal purpose.

REFLECTION

1. How does uncertainty reveal the depth of your faith?
2. Why is generosity a form of trust in God's provision?
3. What does diligent work look like when results are unpredictable?
4. How can joy and reverence coexist in daily life?
5. Why is youth such a sacred but fleeting gift?
6. What helps you live courageously without becoming reckless?

DISCUSSION

1. What modern fears keep Christians from taking faithful risks?
2. How does Ecclesiastes challenge perfectionism or hesitation?
3. What examples show that joy can be holy rather than selfish?
4. How does remembering judgment deepen our enjoyment of life?
5. Why is gratitude the foundation of both wisdom and courage?
6. What habits can help believers live boldly without losing humility?

12

BEFORE THE SILVER CORD BREAKS

ECCLESIASTES 12

Objective: To remember your Creator now and live every day in reverent obedience to him.

INTRODUCTION

A few years before his death, C. S. Lewis wrote to a young student who feared growing old: "Do not let your happiness depend on something you may lose." Lewis had learned what Ecclesiastes teaches—that joy rooted in strength, success, or youth eventually slips away. Real joy must rest in something, or Someone, eternal.

Ecclesiastes 12 is Qohelet's final sermon after a lifetime of searching. He turns from describing life's frustrations to urging a single act of faith: "Remember your Creator in the days of your youth." Memory here is not nostalgia—it's orientation. To remember God means to live every moment in light of his reality and rule. The Teacher knows that forgetfulness is humanity's greatest danger, not ignorance. When we forget God, life becomes mere routine; when we remember him, even aging becomes worship.

The closing verses of this chapter form one of the Bible's most beautiful laments: the trembling limbs, the dimmed eyes, the silent streets—all vivid symbols of the body's decline. Yet Qohelet's tone is not despairing but reverent. He invites readers to see aging, death, and judgment as threads in God's tapestry of meaning. Ecclesiastes ends not in futility but in faith. Our fleeting lives find significance when anchored to the eternal Creator who both gives and receives the breath of life.

EXAMINATION

The call to remember (12:1)

"Remember also your Creator in the days of your youth, before the evil days come and the years draw near of which you will say, 'I have no pleasure in them.'" With this command, Qohelet begins his grand conclusion. The verb "remember" (*zākar*) implies more than recollection—it means to live in faithful awareness of God's presence and authority. To remember the Creator is to orient one's entire life toward him.

The Teacher addresses the young not to exclude the old but because youth is the season of opportunity. Choices made early shape the character that endures later. The "evil days" refer to the hardships of aging—when vitality wanes and joy fades. Wisdom calls for devotion before decline, reverence before regret. To delay faithfulness until life slows down is to misunderstand its purpose. The wise begin early, knowing that the same God who gives youth its energy deserves its allegiance.

The fading of life (12:2–5)

Qohelet paints one of Scripture's most poetic depictions of aging. "Before the sun and the light and the moon and the stars are darkened, and the clouds return after the rain." The imagery of darkened skies and unending storms suggests a season when recovery becomes rare—when one hardship follows another without reprieve.

"In the day when the keepers of the house tremble, and the strong men are bent, and the grinders cease because they are few, and those who look through the windows are dimmed." The metaphors describe the body's decline: trembling limbs ("keepers"), bent shoulders ("strong men"), worn teeth ("grinders"), and fading eyesight ("windows").

"When the doors on the street are shut, and the sound of the grinding is low, and one rises up at the sound of a bird, and all the daughters of song are brought low." Hearing grows faint; sleep becomes restless. Once lively voices lose their tone. "They are afraid also of what is high, and terrors are in the way; the almond tree blossoms, the grasshopper drags itself along, and desire fails, because man is going to his eternal home, and the mourners go about the streets." The white almond blossoms symbolize gray hair; the sluggish grasshopper depicts exhaustion; "desire" (literally "caperberry") no longer stimulates.

Qohelet's language is tender rather than cynical. He dignifies aging as a universal pilgrimage toward eternity. Every metaphor points to mortality's approach—an invitation to gratitude, not despair.

The final moment of life (12:6-7)

"Before the silver cord is snapped, or the golden bowl is broken, or the pitcher is shattered at the fountain, or the wheel broken at the cistern." Four images illustrate death's sudden finality. The silver cord and golden bowl evoke a lamp—the severed cord extinguishes the light. The pitcher and wheel suggest a well—the broken mechanism ends the flow of water. Life's light and breath cease; beauty and function collapse together.

"And the dust returns to the earth as it was, and the spirit returns to God who gave it." Echoing Genesis 2:7, Qohelet reminds readers that life begins and ends in God's hands. Dust speaks of mortality; spirit speaks of divine origin. The two movements—returning to earth and returning to God—sum up human existence. Death is not escape from God but encounter with him.

Qohelet's realism is anchored in reverence. Death, inevitable though it is, remains sacred because it completes the circle of divine creation. The Creator who gave life receives it again.

The refrain of vanity (12:8)

"Vanity of vanities, says the Preacher; all is vanity." The book's opening cry now returns as its echoing conclusion. The Hebrew *hebel*—vapor, breath, mist—captures both the beauty and brevity of life. Qohelet does not use the word to deny meaning but to demand humility. Everything under the sun is transient; permanence belongs only to God.

This refrain frames Ecclesiastes as a meditation on limits. Work, pleasure, wisdom, wealth, and youth—all good gifts—cannot outlast time. The Teacher's repeated observation of vanity is not cynicism but worship. Only the eternal Creator can anchor life's impermanence in meaning.

The purpose of wisdom literature (12:9-12)

Qohelet now steps back, allowing a narrator—perhaps an editor or student—to summarize his method: "Besides being wise, the Preacher also taught the people knowledge, weighing and studying and arranging many proverbs with great care." His wisdom was both intellectual and pastoral. "The Preacher sought to find words of delight, and uprightly he wrote words of truth." Wisdom aims not only to instruct the mind but to move the heart.

"The words of the wise are like goads, and like nails firmly fixed are the collected sayings; they are given by one Shepherd." The metaphor of "goads" (sharp sticks used to drive cattle) shows that wisdom can sting before it guides. "Nails firmly fixed" evoke stability and permanence. The "one Shepherd" alludes to God himself, the ultimate source of wisdom that both prods and anchors his people.

"My son, beware of anything beyond these. Of making many books there is no end, and much study is a weariness of the flesh." The narrator cautions against endless speculation. Wisdom's goal is not accumulation of data but submission to truth. Knowledge without reverence exhausts rather than enlightens. The pursuit of meaning apart from God only multiplies frustration.

The final word (12:13-14)

"The end of the matter; all has been heard. Fear God and keep his commandments, for this is the whole duty of man." The Hebrew phrase literally reads, "for this is the whole of man." Reverence and obedience define what it means to be human. The book's long wrestling with vanity finds resolution not in explanation but in surrender. Wisdom begins where control ends—with awe before God's holiness.

"For God will bring every deed into judgment, with every secret thing, whether good or evil." This closing promise restores moral order to the world's apparent chaos. What seemed unjust or random "under the sun" will be set right "under heaven." Judgment is not merely threat; it is hope—the assurance that life matters because God sees. Life's meaning is not discovered by escaping vanity but by fearing God amid it. To remember the Creator is to live today in light of eternity.

From vanity to reverence

Ecclesiastes 12 completes the Teacher's pilgrimage from frustration to faith. The book that began with "vanity of vanities" closes with "fear God and keep his commandments." The tension of life under the sun remains, but its purpose is clarified. Mortality humbles us, but memory of the Creator sustains us.

Qohelet's final message transcends generations: youth is fleeting, death certain, and wisdom limited—but reverence endures. When we remember our Creator, even life's vapor becomes luminous. To fear God is not to cower in dread but to live in joyful submission, trusting that our fragile days rest securely in his eternal hands.

APPLICATION

1. Remember God before life's distractions dull your heart

Qohelet's command to "remember your Creator in the days of your youth" is a call to early devotion, not late repentance. Memory in Scripture is more than mental recall—it's covenantal faithfulness. To remember God is to center your life around him while your heart is still soft and your energy strong. The Teacher knows how easily comfort, ambition, and age can erode spiritual zeal. Delay breeds indifference. Every stage of life brings new excuses to postpone obedience. Wisdom begins by deciding that today—not someday—belongs to God. The young who live with awareness of their Creator are better prepared for the "evil days" that come. Reverence formed early becomes refuge later. A remembered God becomes a present comfort when strength fades.

2. See aging as a sacred reminder, not a cruel fate

Qohelet's imagery of trembling limbs and dimmed eyes is not mockery—it's mercy. The fading body is God's sermon on humility. Each ache, wrinkle, and weakness reminds us that eternity is near. The world worships youth and hides from decay; Ecclesiastes teaches us to honor it. Aging is not punishment—it's preparation. The body's decline exposes the soul's dependence. For Christians, the "days of darkness" are not empty but expectant, drawing us closer to the God who renews our inner life day by day. Wisdom receives old age as invitation, not interruption. When we view frailty through faith, we see that weakness is the doorway to worship. Remembering the Creator means trusting that even the breaking of our "golden bowl" will end not in futility, but in the hands of the One who formed us.

3. Anchor your purpose in God's Word, not endless speculation

"Of making many books there is no end," the narrator warns. Knowledge alone cannot satisfy the soul. We live in an age of information but poverty of wisdom. The Teacher reminds us that true learning leads to reverence, not pride. Endless pursuit of insight without submission to God only deepens weariness. Scripture, by contrast, gives both truth and rest—it goads us to holiness and anchors us with assurance. The wise guard against distraction by fixing their hearts on what God has revealed rather than obsessing over what he has concealed. Study is good, but surrender is better. Wisdom matures when curiosity bows to worship. Every Christian must eventually trade speculation for obedience, discovering that the fear of the Lord remains the beginning—and the end—of true knowledge.

4. Live every day in light of judgment and grace

Ecclesiastes ends not with despair but with dignity: "Fear God and keep his commandments, for this is the whole of man." Judgment is certain, but for the faithful it is not doom—it is vindication. The God who sees every hidden thing will one day set all things right. That promise turns accountability into hope. To live in light of judgment is to remember that every moment matters and every act echoes in eternity. Yet Christians do not fear condemnation; they stand in grace. The cross has transformed judgment's terror into gratitude. Wisdom therefore walks in reverence and joy—reverence because God is holy, joy because Christ has borne our vanity and given us victory. The end of the matter is simple: the life that fears God the most enjoys him the best.

CONCLUSION

The book of Ecclesiastes ends where all wisdom must—with the fear of God. Life is fleeting, beauty fades, and strength wanes, but the Creator remains faithful. Qohelet's long search for meaning resolves in humble devotion: to remember, to revere, to obey. Vanity has not been erased—it has been redeemed.

Through this ancient voice, God teaches us to live fully yet faithfully under the sun: to find joy in his gifts, to work with purpose, to speak with grace, and to trust his final judgment. Ecclesiastes does not answer every question, but it gives us the right posture—kneeling before the God who turns vapor into victory.

REFLECTION

1. Why does remembering God early in life strengthen faith later?
2. How does Ecclesiastes dignify aging instead of despairing over it?
3. What keeps people from preparing their souls for eternity?
4. Why is Scripture called both a "goad" and a "nail"?
5. How does the certainty of judgment give hope to believers?
6. What does fearing God look like in your everyday choices?

DISCUSSION

1. What does it mean to "remember your Creator" in practical terms?
2. How does this chapter correct our culture's obsession with youth?
3. What wisdom can older Christians offer from their experience of aging?
4. Why is obedience a better foundation than curiosity or speculation?
5. How does the promise of judgment motivate both reverence and joy?
6. In what ways does Ecclesiastes prepare us for the gospel of Christ?

www.ingramcontent.com/pod-product-compliance
Lightning Source LLC
Chambersburg PA
CBHW070155080526
44586CB00015B/2000